© Nusayba and Sumaya Al-Saadoon, 2018

No-Nonsense Arabic: A Practical, To-The-Point Program for Understanding the Arabic of the Quran – Textbook – 3rd Edition

All rights reserved. This book or any portion thereof may not be reproduced, stored in a retrieval system, or transmitted in any form by any means without the express written permission of Nusayba and Sumaya Al-Saadoon.

For comments/questions contact us at no.nonsense.arabic@gmail.com

For more information visit www.qurancoach.org

ISBN: 978-1-7324585-3-6

TABLE OF CONTENTS

MODULE 1: CORE STRUCTURES

Chapter 01: A Map of the Arabic Language 1
Chapter 02: Now in Arabic... Sentences 15
Chapter 03: Now in Arabic... Fragments 22
Chapter 04: Fragments Inside Sentences 35
Chapter 05: Actions: The Missing Element 47
Chapter 06: The Anomalies 59
Chapter 07: The Passive Voice 72

MODULE 2: MORE ON ACTIONS

Chapter 08: Back-to-Back Actions 82
Chapter 09: Bald Actions 91
Chapter 10: Scenario 1: Shaving Words 95
Chapter 11: Scenario 2: Forbidding 98
Chapter 12: Scenario 3: Conditional Sentences 104
Chapter 13: Scenario 4: Commands 110
Chapter 14: Scenario 5: Command-Consequence 118
Chapter 15: Irregular Bald Actions 122
Chapter 16: Trimmed Actions 125

MODULE 3: ADD-ONS

Chapter 17: Emphasis 133
Chapter 18: The واو 141
Chapter 19: Templates 148

MODULE 4: WORD PATTERNS

Chapter 20: The Agent 155
Chapter 21: The Target 162
Chapter 22: Comparatives 167
Chapter 23: Ideas 173

MODULE 5: COMPLEX STRUCTURES

Chapter 24: Complex Nouns 180
Chapter 25: Complex Descriptors 192
Chapter 26: The Emphasizer مِنْ 197

ICON GUIDE

The icons in this book help you locate particular kinds of information that will be of use to you. Use this guide to familiarize yourself with each icon and what it represents.

This icon draws attention to key points in the lesson.

This icon is used to draw attention to common mistakes and confusions to be aware of.

This icon is used for points that may not be central to the concept at hand, but are still important to know

This icon appears throughout the textbook and instructs you as to what drills to complete at what point

This icon appears next to some questions in the margins of your exercise book. It provides tips and clues that will come in handy for translating and understanding ayaat.

This icon marks the reference that is included at the end of each chapter. It includes the formal grammatical terms as well as the Arabic terms for the concepts we are learning. **_You are not required to learn the contents in this section._** It is simply a reference for those who are interested.

This icon marks the summary section that is included at the end of each chapter. It provides a brief summary of the contents in the chapter.

MODULE -1-

CORE STRUCTURES

A study of the seven structures that form the core of Arabic and the foundation of all other linguistic constructs in the language

CHAPTER 01
A MAP OF THE ARABIC LANGUAGE

INTRODUCTION

Knowing your direction and being familiar with a terrain before embarking on a journey can help you move forward with confidence and clarity of mind. Having seen a bird's eye view of the roads before starting helps you understand how each step will bring you closer to your destination. It gives you a clear sense of where you are and where you will be going.

Arabic, to you right now, is unfamiliar territory. This is why you must take the time to get oriented to the lay of the land and the direction you will be going. Doing so will make your journey smooth and easy.

The map that will be presented to you in this chapter will include the core grammar structures upon which all other structures in the language are built. You will first be introduced to these structures in terms that are understandable to you. This means that in your initial exposure to these concepts, the examples and drills will be in English. Soon after, you will learn to recognize and translate the same structures in Arabic.

THE CORE STRUCTURE OF ARABIC - SENTENCES AND FRAGMENTS

There are two types of sentences and five types of fragments in the Arabic language. Almost the entirety of the Arabic language can be traced back to these seven core structures. Once you have been introduced to these seven structures, you will have a good understanding of the layout of the Arabic language as a whole. Having a good understanding of the structure of the language as a whole will make your transition into the actual Arabic infinitely smoother.

Let us begin our study of the seven core structures. We will start with sentences.

TWO TYPES OF SENTENCES

There are two types of sentences in the Arabic language. They are:

- *ACTION SENTENCES* - sentences that contain an action
- *IS SENTENCES* - sentences that contain the word "is" or one of its variants (are/am) and do not contain any action.

Take a look at an example of each type of sentence.

I **ate** pie.

This sentence contains an action; therefore, it is an ACTION SENTENCE.

Pie **is** tasty.

This sentence contains the word "is" and does not contain any action; therefore, it is an IS SENTENCE.

 Go to Chapter 1, Drill #1: Types of Sentences in your exercise book.

Now that you know how to distinguish between the two types of sentences, let us dig deeper into each of the two types. As you have undoubtedly noticed, an *ACTION SENTENCE* contains more than just the action. Likewise, an *IS SENTENCE* contains more than just the word "is". Let us learn about the parts of each of these two types of sentences. We will begin with *ACTION SENTENCES*.

SENTENCE #1: ACTION SENTENCES

An *ACTION SENTENCE* is made up of three parts. They are:

1. *THE ACTION* - the action word (also known as a verb); the thing that is happening
2. *THE DOER* - the person or thing that carries out the action
3. *THE RECEIVER* - the person or thing affected by the action

Let us revisit the previous example and look at it with fresh eyes in light of the new information.

<u>I |ate| a pie</u>.

What is happening? Eating. Therefore "ate" is the action.
Who/what is doing the action of eating? I am. Therefore "I" am the doer.
Who/what is being affected by the action? The pie. Therefore "the pie" is the receiver.

Of the three parts introduced above, there are two that a sentence needs, and there is one that it optional. Every *ACTION SENTENCE* must have an action and a doer to be considered grammatically complete. The receiver, however, is not an integral part of an *ACTION SENTENCE*, but it appears often.

Take a look at the example below.

<u>The tree |fell|</u>.

What is happening? Falling. Therefore "fell" is the action.
What/who is doing the action of falling? The tree is. Therefore "tree" is the doer.
Who/what is being affected by action? Nothing. There is no receiver in this sentence, <u>YET it is still considered a complete sentence!</u>

 Go to Chapter 1, Drill #2A - Action Sentences in your exercise book.

SENTENCE #2: IS SENTENCES

An *IS SENTENCE* is made up of two parts. They are:

1. *BEFORE IS* - comes before the is/am/are and introduces the topic at hand

2. *AFTER IS* - comes after the is/am/are and gives information about the topic

Let us revisit the previous example and look at it with fresh eyes in light of the new information.

Pie **is** tasty.

The BEFORE IS (pie) is the main topic of discussion. The AFTER IS (tasty) gives information about that topic.

 Go to Chapter 1, Drill #2B - Is Sentences in your exercise book.

Now that we have learned to label both types of sentences, let's mix it up.

 Go to Chapter 1, Drill #2C - Mixed Practice in your exercise book.

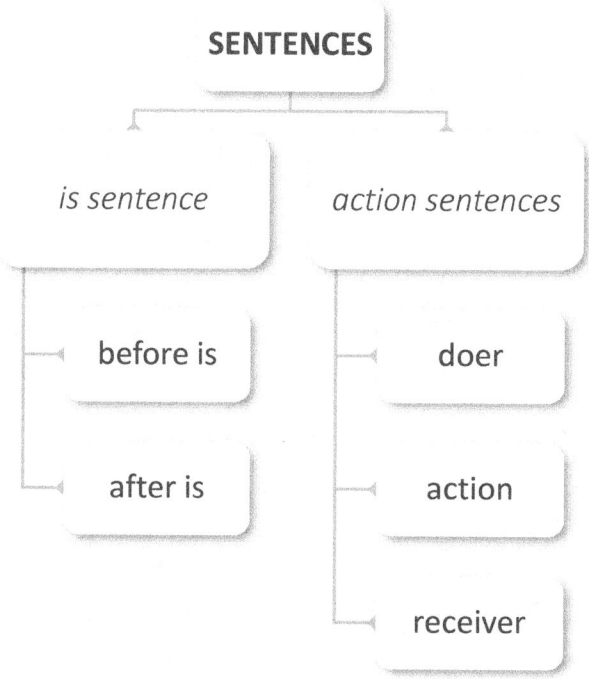

FRAGMENTS

INTRODUCTION

Remember that there are seven core structures that make up the basic map of Arabic, two of which are sentences, and five of which are fragments. We have studied the sentences. It is now time to study the fragments.

You may have noticed that the sentences from the previous section were exceedingly simple. Each part of the sentence (doer, receiver, etc.) was always made up of only one word. In reality, most sentences are often more complex. The parts of a sentence are often made up, not just of one word, but of a string of words.

These strings of words are known as fragments. A fragment is a string of words that cannot stand alone. Fragments do not convey complete thoughts like sentences do.

The parts of the sentences you were introduced to, namely the DOER, RECEIVER, BEFORE IS, and AFTER IS, often appear as fragments. Think of these four sentence parts as buckets that are capable of carrying a single word or of carrying a string of words - a fragment.

Before we study the different fragments and the roles that they play in sentences, let us make sure that we understand what a fragment is.

 Go to Chapter 1, Drill #3: Sentences vs Fragments in your exercise book.

THE FIVE FRAGMENTS

There are five fragments in the Arabic language. A fragment, by definition, cannot stand alone. As such, it always appears as part of something larger. It always appears within a sentence. For this reason, as we study each fragment, we will make a point to look at it in a larger context, just as it would occur in a natural linguistic setting.

FRAGMENT #1: POSSESSIVE

The possessive form shows a relationship of belonging between two or more things – that is, that someone has something. In every possessive fragment, there is at least one owner and one item. Both the owner and the item will be nouns.

Take a look at the following examples.

owner ← **mom**'s **unicycle** → item

Does mom have a unicycle or does the unicycle have a mom? Mom has a unicycle; therefore, "mom" is the owner. That makes the "unicycle" the item.

Note that the item does not have to be a phsyical, tangible item as in the example below.

item ← **the smell** of **the pasta** → owner

Does pasta have a smell or does smell have pasta? Pasta has a smell; therefore, "pasta" is the owner. That makes "smell" the item.

owner ← **my** **ears** → item

Do I have ears or do ears have me? I have ears; therefore, "I" am the owner. That makes "ears" the item.

 Go to Chapter 1, Drill #4A - Owner and Item in your exercise book.

POSSESSIVE CHAINS

Sometimes multiple possessive fragments are strung together. When this happens, it is possible for one word to act both as the owner and the item. We call these possessive chains.

owner + item
↓

item ← **the struggle** of **the lions** of **the Sahara** → owner

The struggle belongs to the lions and the lions belong to the Sahara. This means that the lion is both the owner and the item in this fragment. They possess the struggle and are the possession of the Sahara.

6

Go to Chapter 1, Drill #4B - Possessive Chains in your exercise book.

POSSESSIVES IN CONTEXT

As mentioned previously, a fragment cannot stand alone. Take a look at some examples of these same fragments being used in a natural environment.

What is happening? Breaking. Therefore "broke" is the action.
What is doing the action of breaking? Mom's unicycle. Therefore the possessive fragment "mom's unicycle" is playing the role of the doer. The entire fragment is acting as a doer for the action "broke".

What is happening? Loving. Therefore "love" is the action.
Who is doing the action of loving? I am. Therefore, "I" am the doer.
What do I love? The smell of pasta. Therefore the possessive fragment "the smell of pasta" is playing the role of the receiver. The entire fragment is acting as a receiver for the action "love".

These **are** my ears.
possessive

The possessive fragment "my ears" is playing the role of the AFTER IS, or in this case the AFTER ARE.

Just like normal possessive fragments, possessive chains cannot stand alone. They also only appear in a larger sentence.

<u>The struggle of the lions of the Sahara</u> |amazes| <u>me</u>.

          possessive #1   possessive #2

The possessive chain in this sentence is playing the role of the doer. What is doing the action of "amazing"? It is "the struggle of the lions of the Sahara".

 Go to Chapter 1, Drill #4C - Role of Possessives in your exercise book.

FRAGMENT #2: DESCRIPTIVE

A descriptive fragment is made up of a word that is being described and the word that is describing it. It is, in other words, made up of a noun and an adjective. Compare this to possessives in which you have two nouns.

Take a look at the examples below.

description ← **<u>fresh</u> <u>milk</u>** → described

description ← **<u>green</u> <u>pants</u>** → described

description ← **<u>fluffy</u> <u>kitten</u>** → described

Just like possessive fragments, descriptive fragment appear within larger sentences. Can you try placing the fragments above in a sentence?

 Go to Chapter 1, Drill #5: Descriptive Fragments in your exercise book.

FRAGMENT #3: POINTING

The pointers in English are: this, these, that, and those. A pointing fragment is made up of a pointer and a noun.

pointer ← |those| blueberries → noun

pointer ← |that| bubble tea → noun

pointer ← |this| phone call → noun

Just like possessive and descriptive fragments, pointer fragments play a larger role in a sentence. Try placing each of the fragments above in a sentence. See if you can make each play a different role.

 Go to Chapter 1, Drill #6: Pointer Scavenger Hunt in your exercise book.

FRAGMENT #4: SENTENCE STARTERS

The sentence starters are: certainly, that, as though, maybe, and if only/perhaps. A sentence starter fragment is made up of a sentence starter (one of the words mentioned above) followed by a noun.

sentence starter ← |Certainly|, you (...are obsessed)
↓
noun

sentence starter ← |If only| he (...was faster)
↓
noun

sentence starter ← |Perhaps| it (...is closer than you think)
↓
noun

While sentence started appear at the head of a sentence, they are an "auxiliary" feature of sorts. While they do add meaning, they can be removed, leaving behind a grammatically sound sentence.

~~Certainly,~~ you are obsessed with cats.

~~If only~~ he was a little bit faster.

~~Perhaps~~ it was just a mistake.

FRAGMENT #5: TIME-LOCATION-DIRECTION-RELATION PHRASE

Words like *after*, *above*, *toward*, and *with* are known as time-location-direction-relation words because they give information about one of these four things. A time-location-direction-relation phrase (TLDR phrase for short) is made up of a TLDR word and a noun that follows it directly.

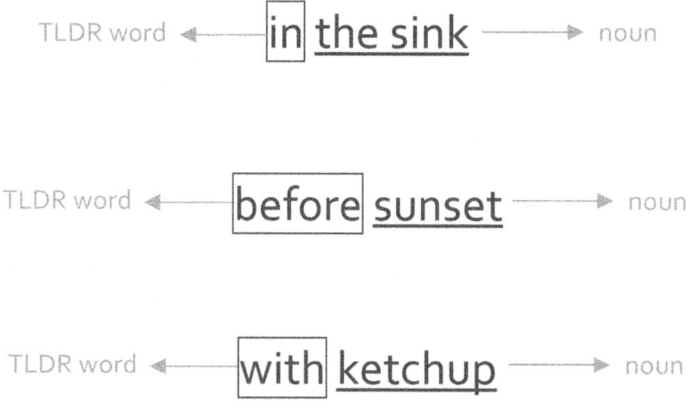

Note that while a TLDR phrase can appear as a BEFORE IS or AFTER IS, it does not appear as a doer or receiver. TLDR phrases are most often extra parts that appear in addition to the main parts of a sentence and provide additional information about time or location.

FRAGMENT CHAINS

A fragment is a chain of words. Sometimes these chains link to each other to form longer chains. When two or more fragments come together, the structure is known as a fragment chain. Fragment chains can be made up of any number of the five fragments in many different sequences. As is the case with normal fragments, fragment chains cannot stand alone. They always appear in a sentence.

<u>As long as the links between fragments continue, they are treated as a single chain or a single unit, and will -- as a unit -- play a single role in the sentence.</u>

I have a brother and my brother has a room -> possessive chain

The room is described as dirty -> descriptive fragment

"In" tells me about the location -> TLDR phrase

"With" tells me about relation -> TLDR phrase

"That" is a pointer word -> pointer fragment

The soup is described as delicious -> descriptive fragment

It is also possible for fragments to be linked together using a connecting word like "and". When fragments or fragment chains are linked together using a connector word, they are treated as a single unit and will play a single role in the sentence.

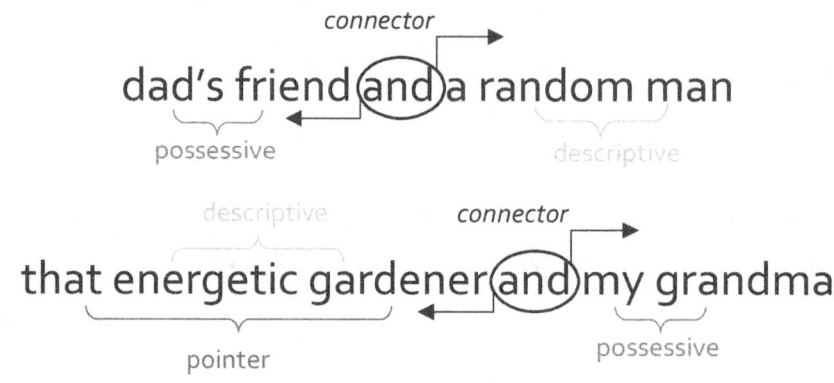

 *Go to Chapter 1, Drill #7: Fragment Chain Labelling in your exercise book.*

Though fragment chains are longer than normal fragments, they are still incomplete thoughts. This means that they also play a role in a larger sentence. Can you place these fragment chains in a sentence?

 Go to Chapter 1, Drill #8: Bringing it All Together in your exercise book.

IN A NUTSHELL

IS SENTENCES

- BEFORE IS
- AFTER IS

ACTION SENTENCES

① THE ACTION
② THE DOER
③ THE RECEIVER

these roles can be one word or a fragment

- THE FRAGMENTS -

① POSSESSIVE

Shows a relationship of belonging between two or more things.
- noun + noun
- item + owner
- can come in chains (item + owner-item + owner)

② DESCRIPTIVE

Made up of a word that is being described and the word that is describing it
- described (noun) + description (adjective)

③ POINTER

A pointing fragment is used to point at someone/something..
- pointer + noun

④ SENTENCE STARTERS

Sentence starters are: certainly, that, as though, maybe, and if only/perhaps.
- sentence starter + noun
- comes at the start of the sentence
- auxiliary feature, can be removed

⑤ TLDR PHRASE

TLDR words are words that indicate time, location, or direction
- TLDR word + noun

***does not necessarily fit into a specific role!

FRAGMENT CHAINS

A fragment is a chain of words. Sometimes these chains link to each other to form longer chains. When two or more fragments come together, the structure is known as a fragment chain.

It is also possible for fragments to be linked together using a connecting word like "and".

OUR TERM	FORMAL TERM	ARABIC TERM
is-sentence	nominal sentence	جُمْلَة اِسْمِيَّة
action sentence	verbal sentence	جُمْلَة فِعْلِيَّة
action	verb	فِعْل
doer	subject	فَاعِل
receiver	direct object	مَفْعُول بِهِ
before-is	topic	مُبْتَدَأ
after-is	predicate	خَبَر/مُتَعَلِّق بِالخَبَر[1]
possessive	genitive construction	إِضَافَة
owner	construct state	مُضَاف
item	governed noun	مُضَاف إِلَيْهِ
descriptive	noun and adjective	المَوْصُوف وَالصِّفَة
TLDR phrase	prepositional phrase	جَارّ ومَجْرُور/ظَرْف[2]
pointer	demonstrative pronoun	اِسْم الإِشَارَة
pointer's noun	-	مُشَار إِلَيْهِ

[1] When a TLDR phrase comes in an *IS SENTENCE*, it is called متعلق بالخبر

[2] TLDR words that end in a ‍َ are called ظرف, those that don't are called حرف جر

CHAPTER 02
Now in Arabic... Sentences

INTRODUCTION

Now that you have a good understanding of the two sentences and five fragments that make up the core structure of Arabic, it is time to learn the Arabic versions of these structures. We will proceed in the same sequence, studying sentences, then fragments, then looking at how fragments fit into sentences.

ACTION SENTENCES

RECOGNIZING THE PARTS

Recall that an action sentence is made up of an action, a doer, and sometimes a receiver. You were able to identify these three parts in English because:

- ✓ You already understand the language
- ✓ Action sentences in English always come in the set sequence of doer -> action -> receiver

In Arabic, however, the sequencing of action sentences is flexible and the meaning might not be instantly apparent to you. This means that you must employ a different strategy for identifying the parts. Luckily, there is a very systematic, reliable method of identification.

1. **ACTION** - In Arabic action sentences, the action is always the first word in the sentence

Though the position of the action is fixed, the doer and receiver often swap places with each other. For this reason, the doer and receiver cannot be identified based on sequence. ***The doer and receiver are identified based on a label that is tacked on to the end of the word.*** The doer and receiver each have a unique set of labels by which they can be identified.

2. **DOER** - If you see any of the following labels attached to the end of the word, it is a doer. You will notice that there are four separate labels for the same function. This is because different labels are used depending on the *number* of doers or the *gender* of the doer(s). The *standard* label can appear on words of any number or gender. When you see a *standard* label, you will be able to correctly identify the number and gender of the word by knowing your voabulary.

اتٌ / اتُ	وْنَ	انِ	ءُ / ءٌ
PLURAL (WOMEN/INANIMATE OBJECTS)	**PLURAL**	**PAIR**	**STANDARD**

3. **RECEIVER** - If you see any of the following labels attached to the end of the word, it is a receiver. You will notice that there are four separate labels for the same function. This is because different labels are used depending on the *number* of receivers or the *gender* of the receiver(s). The *standard* label can appear on words of any number or gender. When you see a *standard* label, you will be able to correctly identify the number and gender of the word by knowing your voabulary.

اتِ / اتٍ	ِيْنَ	َيْنِ	ءَ / ءً
PLURAL (WOMEN/INANIMATE OBJECTS)	**PLURAL**	**PAIR**	**STANDARD**

Take a look at the following examples.

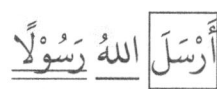

Allah sent a prophet.

Notice that the doer is marked by a ُ label and that the receiver is marked by a َ label.

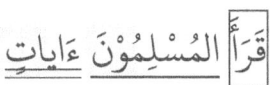

The Muslims read verses.

Notice that the doer is marked by a وْنَ label and that the receiver is marked by a اتِ label. Notice also that the doer and receiver are translated as plural because of their plural label (وْنَ / اتِ).

 Go to Chapter 2, Drill #1: Recognizing Labels.

When you see a ﹷ, make sure that it's not just part of a larger يْنَ/وْنَ label before rushing to conclusions. When you see a ﹻ, makes sure that it's not just part of a larger اتْ اتِ label before rushing to conclusions.

Now that you know how to identify the action, doer, and receiver, it's time to tackle full sentences. Remember, the action is the first word in the sentence. The doer and receiver are identified based on the labels at the end of the word.

 Go to Chapter 2, Drill #2A – Labelling Action Sentences.

TRANSLATING ACTION SENTENCES

Remember that in English, the standard sequence of an action sentence is doer -> action -> receiver. The sequence in Arabic is different. When translating, however, it is important that the translation makes sense in the target language. This is why the elements should be translated according to what is natural in English. Use the following guide to help you translate from Arabic to English:

1. Translate the doer

2. Translate the action

3. Translate the receiver

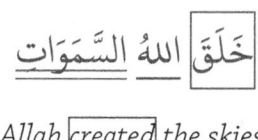

<u>Allah</u> [created] <u>the skies</u>.

👉 *Go to Chapter 2, Drill #2B – Translating Action Sentences.*

WHEN THE RECEIVER IS A PRONOUN

When the words *me, you, us, him, her, it,* or *them* act as a receiver, the rules change a bit. These words are known as pronouns. **When a pronoun appears as a receiver, it attaches itself directly to the action.** When a pronoun attaches to an action, you can always safely say that it is a receiver. A pronoun attaching to an action is its way of showing that it is a receiver. For this reason, pronouns do not require any additional labels. **They do not take any of the standard receiver labels.**

Take a look at the example below.

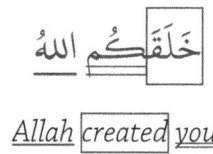

<u>Allah</u> [created] <u>you</u>.

Notice that the pronoun has attached itself directly to the action and does not have any of the standard receiver label, yet it is translated as the receiver.

👉 *Go to Chapter 2, Drill #3 – Pronouns as Receivers.*

IS SENTENCES

Recall that an *IS SENTENCE* is made up of two parts: the *BEFORE IS* and the *AFTER IS*. **The key difference between an "is sentence" in English and an "is sentence" in Arabic is that the word "is" does not exist in Arabic. The "is" is invisible.**

Arabic IS SENTENCES, in their simplest form, are made up of two words. The BEFORE IS comes first and the AFTER IS follows.

Since there is no IS in Arabic you must insert it into your translation when moving from Arabic to English.

واللهُ | قديرٌ

*Allah **is** capable.*

Though these IS SENTENCES are very simple as they are made up of only two words, it is important to remember that all of the fragment types we will learn are *also* made up of two words. A key observation that will help you distinguish an IS SENTENCE from these fragment types is the following:

1. The BEFORE IS is specific (referring to something particular)
2. The AFTER IS is general (referring to something generic)

Notice how this applies to the example above. The word الله is specific. The word قدير is general. When translating, simply place the IS between the general word and the specific word.

Keeping this key observation in mind will help you recognize IS SENTENCE, so let's practice differentiating between general words and specific words.

 *Go to Chapter 2, Drill #4: General vs Specific.*

Now that we know how to differentiate between general and specific words, let's practice translating IS SENTENCES.

 *Go to Chapter 2, Drill #5 – Translating Is Sentences.*

There are two types of sentences: *ACTION SENTENCES* and *IS SENTENCES*.

ACTION SENTENCES

- **ACTION** is the first word in the sentence

- **DOER** has one of the following labels: ءُ/ءَ   انِ   ونَ   اتُ / اتٌ

- **RECEIVER** has one of the following labels: ءَ/ءًا   يْنِ   ـِيْنَ   اتِ / اتٍ

    o Pronouns that attach directly to the **ACTION** will always be a receiver

IS SENTENCES

- **BEFORE IS** is specific

- **AFTER IS** is general

OUR TERM	FORMAL TERM	ARABIC TERM
doer label	nominative	رَفْع
receiver label	accusative	نَصْب
pronoun	"	ضَمِيْر
attached pronoun	possessive pronoun/object pronoun[1]	ضَمِيْر مُتَّصِل
general	indefinite	نَكِرَة
specific	definite	مَعرِفَة

[1] it is an object pronoun when attached to an action as a receiver, and a possessive pronoun when attached to a noun as an owner

CHAPTER 03
Now in Arabic... Fragments

INTRODUCTION

Remember that parts of a sentence are often made up of more than one word - they are made up of fragments. In order to study sentences that contain fragments, we must first learn to recognize the five fragments.

FRAGMENT #1: POSSESSIVE

PARTS OF A POSSESSIVE FRAGMENT

The possessive form shows a relationship of belonging between two or more words and is made up of an *ITEM* and an *OWNER*.

There are three things to know about recognizing the possessive form in Arabic:

1. The *ITEM* always comes first
2. The *ITEM* is general and the *OWNER* is specific
3. Both are nouns

Let's take a look at some examples.

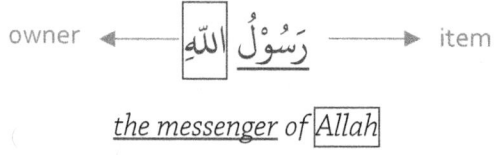

the messenger of Allah

The word رسول (item) comes first.

The word رسول (item) is general, the word الله (owner) is specific.

Both words are nouns.

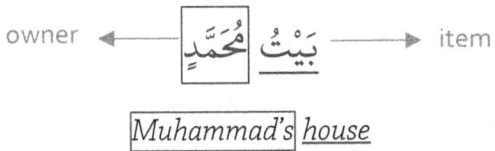

owner ← → item

Muhammad's house

The word بيت (item) comes first.

The word بيت (item) is general, the word محمد (owner) is specific

Both words are nouns.

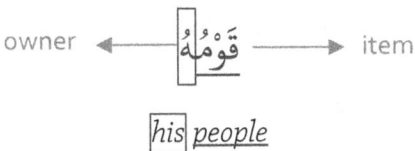

owner ← → item

his people

The word قوم (item) comes first.

The word قوم (item) is general, the word ه (owner) is specific

Both words are nouns.

notice that when the owner is a pronoun, it attaches directly to the item

TRANSLATING POSSESSIVE FRAGMENTS

There are two ways that possessive fragments appear in English.

1. **Owner's item**

    e.g. Allah's messenger

    An apostrophe + s is placed on the owner. The item follows.

2. **Item of owner**

    e.g. The messenger of Allah

    The word "of" is placed between the item and the owner.

You may use either of these two methods when translating from Arabic to English. Now, remember that in Arabic, the item comes first and the owner comes second.

Let's give it a try.

 Go to Chapter 3, Drill #1 - Labelling and Translating Possessive Fragments.

Recall that sometimes multiple possessive fragments are strung together. The same rules mentioned above apply, with one minor difference: The last word is specific and every word that comes before it is general. When you see two general nouns, check for a specific noun after them. Chances are, you are looking at a possessive chain. In other words, a possessive chain is recognized by general + general + specific.

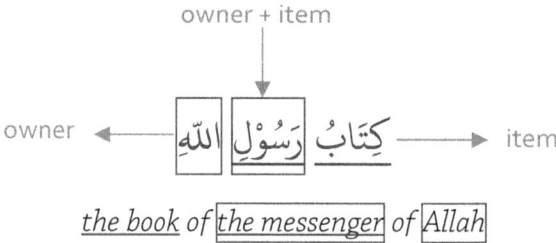

Notice that the words كتاب and رسول are general and the word الله is specific.

In other words, the last word is specific, and every word that comes before that is general.

 Go to Chapter 3, Drill #1B - Labelling and Translating Possessive Fragments Chains.

FRAGMENT #2: DESCRIPTIVE

A descriptive fragment is made up of a word that is being described and the word that is describing it.

There are three things to know about recognizing the descriptive form in Arabic:

1. A descriptive fragment is made up of a noun and a description

2. The noun comes first and the description comes second

3. Both the noun and description are either **_both general or both specific_**

description ← رَبٌّ غَفُورٌ → described

<u>a forgiving</u> Lord

The word رب (Lord) is a noun and the word غفور (forgiving) is a description.

The noun (رب) comes first and the description (غفور) comes second.

Both words are general.

description ← الْقَوْمَ الظَّالِمِيْنَ → described

<u>the oppressive</u> nation

The word القوم (the nation) is a noun and the word الظالمين (the oppressive) is a description.

The noun (القوم) comes first and the description (الظالمين) comes second.

Both words are specific.

 Go to Chapter 3, Drill #2: Descriptive Fragments.

DIFFERENTIATING BETWEEN POSSESSIVE AND DESCRIPTIVE

Both possessive and descriptive fragments involve two words coming together. These two fragment types translate very differently. As such, it is important that you do not confuse them.

There is a simple method you can use to differentiate between the two. Recall that in a possessive fragment, the first word is general and the second is specific. Now recall that in a descriptive fragment the two words match in generality or specificity.

To distinguish between possessive and descriptive, simply check the generality/specificity of the two words. If they match, it is descriptive. If they mismatch, it is possessive.

Also remember that a possessive fragment is made up of two nouns. A descriptive fragment is made up of a noun and an adjective. Make sure you memorize the adjectives in your vocabulary so that you can distinguish between nouns and adjectives.

Remember that in a possessive chain, only the last word is specific. This means that first two words in a possessive chain are general. Make sure not to confuse possessive chains with descriptives! Even though both may contain two general words in a row, REMEMBER that possessives are made up of 2 or more nouns. Descriptives are made up of a noun and an adjective.

Here's a cheat sheet:

General + General	= descriptive	noun + adjective
Specific + Specific	= descriptive	
General + Specific	= possessive	noun + noun
Specific + General	= is sentence	

  Go to Chapter 3, Drill #3: Differentiating Between Fragments.

FRAGMENT #3: POINTING

A pointing fragment is made up of a pointer and a noun that follows it directly. The pointers in Arabic are listed in the Chapter 3 vocabulary.

The only additional thing you need to know about pointing fragments in Arabic is that *the word that follows the pointer directly will always have an ال. If there is no ال, it is not a fragment.* If there is no ال, there is *no relationship* between the two words.

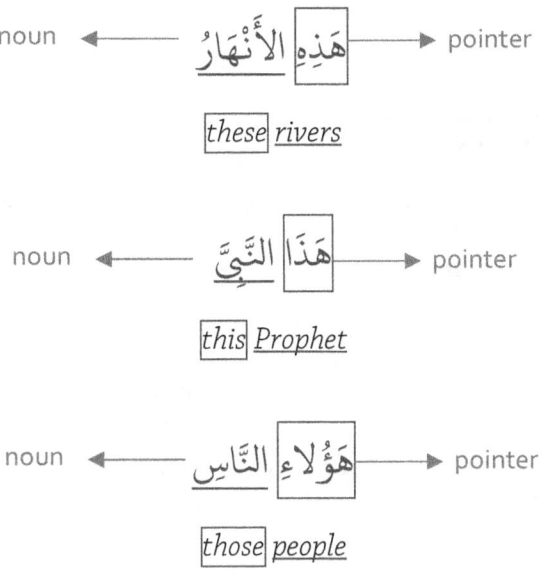

Go to Chapter 3, Drill #4: Pointer Fragments.

FRAGMENT #4: SENTENCE STARTERS

Sentence starter fragments are made up of a sentence starter and a noun that follows is directly. The sentence starters in Arabic listed in Chapter 3 vocabulary.

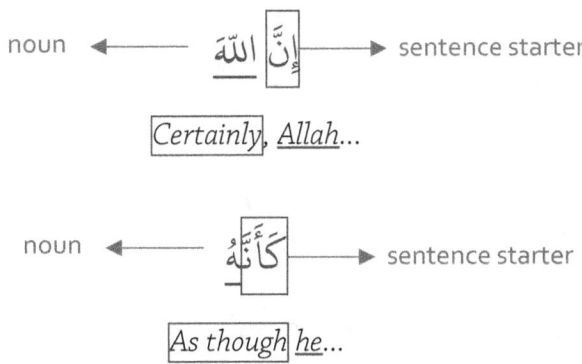

Notice that the pronoun attaches directly to the sentence starter.

Note that when the attached pronouns نا and ني attach to the sentence starter إنَّ there are two possible scenarios. Either the ن in the two words merge, or they do not. This is why you will sometimes see إنِّي/أنَّا in the Quran, and at other times you will see إنَّني/أنَّنا. They translate the same way.

Go to Chapter 3, Drill #5: Sentence Starters.

FRAGMENT #5: TLDR PHRASE

Remember that TLDR stands for **t**ime, **l**ocation, **d**irection, and **r**elation. A TLDR word is a word that tells you about one of these four things. Words like *after*, *above*, *toward*, and *with* are TLDR words because they give information about time, location, direction, and relation. TLDR phrases in Arabic are made up of a TLDR word and a noun that follows it directly.

The Arabic TLDR words are listed in Chapter 3 & 7 vocabulary. Focus on the words from Chapter 3 for now!

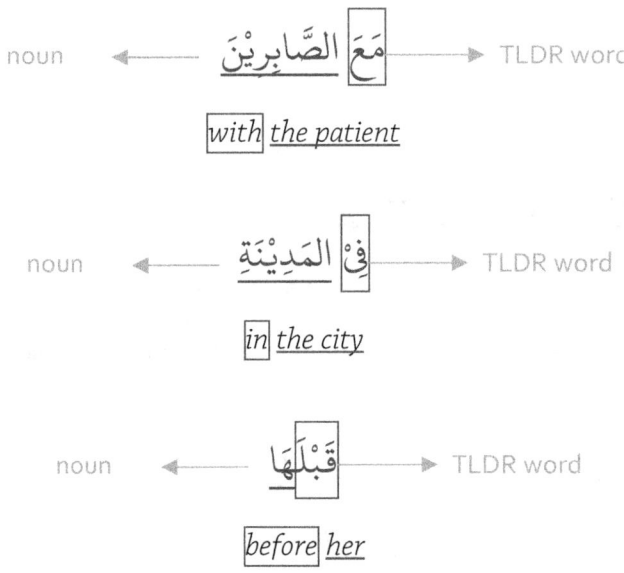

Notice that the pronoun attaches directly to the TLDR word.

There are three propositions that change ever so slightly when a pronoun attaches to them:

1. لِ: the ـِ becomes ـَ

2. على and إلى: the ى becomes a ي

PRONOUN + لـ	NORMAL NOUN + لـ	PRONOUN + على/إلى	NORMAL NOUN + على/إلى
لَهُ	لِقَوْمِهِ	عَلَيْهِ	عَلَى الأَرْضِ
لَنا	لِأَجَلٍ	إِلَيْنا	إِلَى المَوْتِ
لَكُمْ	لِمَسْجِدٍ	عَلَيْهِمْ	عَلَى البَحْرِ

Also note that when لـ attaches to a word that begins with الـ, the ا disappears. This leaves you with two لـ in a row.

$$لِـ + القَوْمُ \longrightarrow لِلْقَوْمِ$$

$$لِـ + اللّٰهُ \longrightarrow لِلّٰهِ$$

 Go to Chapter 3, Drill #6: TLDR Phrases.

FRAGMENT CHAINS

Recall that fragments can come together to form fragment chains. The rules of each fragment do not change when it becomes part of a chain. This means that the same methods of recognition for each fragment can be used.

It is important to note, however, that when fragments link, **the same word can be shared by two fragments.**

sentence starter

إِنَّ رَسُولَ اللّٰهِ

possessive

Certainly, the messenger of Allah
sentence starter   possessive

Notice that the word رسول is shared by two fragments. It is simultaneously acting as the second word in a sentence starter and the item in a possessive fragment.

Because the same word can be shared by two fragments, it is imperative to overlap words when working through a fragment chain. In a fragment chain, every word that is sandwiched between two words will be in a relationship with both.

If you were to work through the fragment chain above, for example, you would first determine the relationship between the first two words: إنَّ رسول. Then you would determine the relationship between the second and third words: رسول الله. The word رسول gets analyzed twice because it is in between two words.

The word في is related to the word هذه because it is a TLDR word and its noun.
The word هذه is related to the word القرية because it is a pointer followed by a noun with ال.
The word القرية is related to the word الكبيرة because it is a specfic noun + a specific description.

 Go to Chapter 3, Drill 7A – Identifying and Translating Fragment Chains.

DESCRIBING + POSSESSION

There is one fragment combination in particular that is unique and deserves special attention. That is the descriptive + possessive combination. It is possible to give a possessive fragment a description as in the example below:

In the fragment above, "his beard" is being described as "black". That makes "his beard" the described and "black" the adjective/descriptor. The described, in this case, however, is a possessive fragment, "his" acting as the owner and "beard" acting as the item.

This fragment combination is unique in that the descriptor is not just associated with the *word* before it. It is associated with the entire *fragment* before it.

Notice that, in the Arabic, there is an ال on the adjective, but not on the noun. The rule that both parts of a descriptive fragment must either be general or specific still holds. The reason the first word does not have an ال on it is that "her house" is already specific. It is not talking about a random house, but a specific one. Because it is already specific, there is no need to add an ال.

Keep an eye out for this fragment combination as it is often overlooked because of its unique structure.

 Go to Chapter 3, Drill 7B – Describing Possessive Fragments.

MORE ON FRAGMENTS - RELATIONSHIPS & BREAKS

The study of the five fragments is essentially a study of the types of relationships a word can be in. If a word is not part of a fragment, it is not in a relationship. When two words are not in a relationship, we call this a **_break_**. A break indicates the end of a fragment or fragment chain.

There are three scenarios in which breaks occur. We call this the list of "easy breaks" because they make finding your breaks easy!

A break will always occur:

1. **_between a specific word and a general word_**

    Remember that general + specific makes a possessive fragment. When the two words match in generality or specificity, that makes a descriptive fragment.
    Notice, however, that there is no fragment scenario that involves specific + general. No fragment means no relationship, which means that there is a break.

2. **_between two specific nouns_**

    The only fragment involving two nouns is a possessive, but to make a possessive fragment, the nouns have to be general + specific. Although descriptives can involve two specific words, the first is a noun and the second must be an adjective. There is no fragment scenario that involves two specific nouns. No fragment means no relationship, which means that there is a break.

3. **_before a TLDR word_**

    A TLDR can never be related to what comes before it – only to the word coming after it. This means that it always starts a new fragment chain. There is always a break before a TLDR word.

FRAGMENT	RECOGNITION METHOD
POSSESSIVE	-item (first word) • will always be a general noun -owner (second word) • will be a specific noun -possessive chains: general + general + specific -translates as "owner's item" or "item of owner"
DESCRIPTIVE	-both words match in specificity or generality -first word is a noun, second is an adjective -when describing a possessive fragment, the description will have an ال -in Arabic, the noun comes first and the description comes second. When translating to English, description is first and noun is second.
POINTER	memorize pointer words • always followed by a word with ال
SENTENCE STARTER	memorize sentence starters
TLDR PHRASE	memorize TLDR words

EASY BREAKS:
1. between a specific word and a general word
2. between two specific nouns
3. before a TLDR word

OUR TERM	FORMAL TERM	ARABIC TERM
possessive fragment	possessive form	إِضَافَة
item	construct state	مُضَاف
owner	governed noun	مُضَاف إِلَيْهِ
descriptive fragment	noun – adjective	المَوْصُوف وَالصِّفَة/النَّعْت وَالمَنْعُوْت
described	noun	المَوْصُوف/المَنْعُوْت
description	adjective	الصِّفَة/النَّعْت
TLDR word	preposition	ظَرْف/حَرْف جَرّ[1]
pointer fragment	-	اِسْم الإِشَارَة وَالمُشَار إِلَيْهِ
pointer	demonstrative pronoun	اِسْم الإِشَارَة
pointer's noun	-	المُشَار إِلَيْهِ
sentence starter	accusative particles	حَرْف نَصْب/حَرْف مُشَبَّه بِالفِعْل
sentence starter's noun	-	اِسْم "إِنَّ/أَنَّ/كَأَنَّ/لَيْتَ/لَـكِنَّ/لَعَلَّ"[2]
doer label	nominative case	رَفْع
receiver label	accusative case	نَصْب

[1] TLDR words that end in a ـَ are called ظرف, those that don't are called حرف جر

[2] the name varies depending on which sentence starter is being used

CHAPTER 04
Fragments Inside Sentences

INTRODUCTION

We have studied simple sentences in Arabic and we have studied fragments. It is now time to merge the two. Remember that the parts of a sentence are often made up of more than one word. They are made up of fragments.

Though we had to take the time to learn each Arabic fragment in isolation, practically speaking, fragments never appear in isolation. We also learned to recognize fragment chains, but even chains do not appear in isolation. Though being able to recognize and translate them in isolation is a prerequisite to being able to do the same within a sentence, each skill is useless without the other, so make sure to take the contents of this chapter seriously!

We have two tasks ahead of us in our study of sentences that contain fragments. They are:

- **MACRO ANALYSIS** - Determining the larger parts of a sentence

    o *ACTION, DOER, DETAIL* in a *ACTION SENTENCE*

    o *BEFORE IS* and *AFTER IS* in an *IS SENTENCE*

- **MICRO ANALYSIS** - Determining the fragments contained within those parts

To translate a sentence properly from Arabic to English, you have to be able to do both macro and micro analysis. Below are some example of sentences labeled using both methods of analysis.

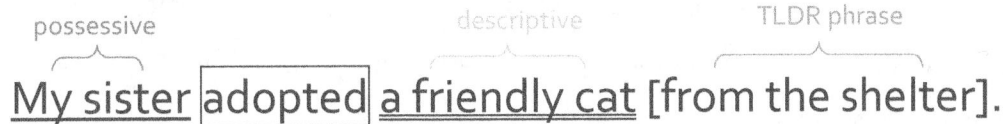

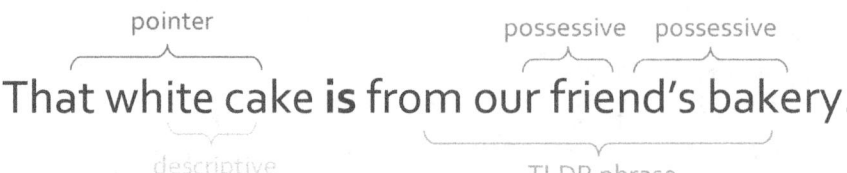

Since you have learned both simple sentences and fragments, this chapter will not contain new information. It will simply give you tips on how to navigate the merged version of what you have already studied as separate elements.

ACTION SENTENCES

Recall that the action is the first word in an ACTION SENTENCE. The doer and receiver are recognizable based on the labels that appear on the end of the word.

Our task, now that we know that the doer and receiver are not always just one word, is to determine the **boundaries** of the doer and the **boundaries** of the receiver. In other words, we now need to figure out where the doer and receiver start and where they end.

For labelling ACTION SENTENCES, we use what we call the BREAK AND SORT METHOD. We start by finding all the **relationships and breaks** between words. Each break indicated the end of one **boundary** and the start of another. Once we have found our breaks and boundaries, we **sort** the fragment chains into either the doer role or the receiver role.

These are the exact steps for the break and sort method. <u>*Pay close attention! This is the method we will be using from here on out!*</u>

1. **Box off the action**

    The action is always the first word in the sentence. We box it off because it is never part of a fragment.

2. **Find all the breaks**

    Go word by word and determine whether each word is related to the next. Once you have found the end of a fragment chain, mark that you have found a **break**. Remember our list of EASY BREAKS!

3. **Sort the parts of the sentence**

    Remember that we determine the parts of the sentence in Arabic using word **labels**.

Check the first word in the fragment for a *DOER LABEL* or a *RECEIVER LABEL*. If the first word has the *DOER LABEL*, then the entire fragment is your *DOER*. If it has the *RECEIVER LABEL*, then the entire fragment is your *RECEIVER*.

4. **Translate accordingly**

   Remember, the sequence for translating an *ACTION SENTENCE* is *DOER* -> *ACTION* -> *RECEIVER* -> *TLDR*.

Let us apply these methods to a sentence.

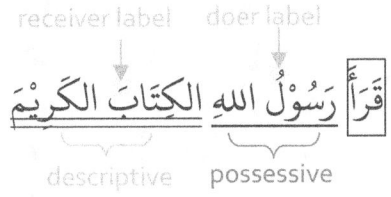

The messenger of Allah recited *the noble book*.

We started off by boxing off the action.

We know that رسول الله are connected because it is a general noun + specfic noun, so it is a possessive fragment.

The word الله and الكتاب cannot be connected because they are both specific nouns, which is an easy break. We have found our first break.

الكتاب is connected to الكريم because it is a specific noun + a specific description.

Now let's sort.

The word رسول has a doer label, therefore the entire fragment (رسول الله) is the doer.

The word الكتاب has a receiver label, therefore the entire fragment (الكتاب الكريم) is the receiver.

Note the sequence of the translation is doer -> action -> receiver.

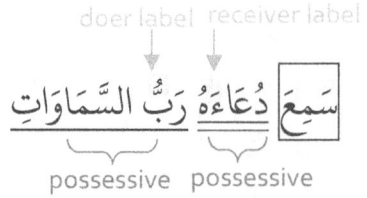

The Lord of the heavens heard *his prayer*.

We start by boxing off the action.

We know that دعاءه *are connected because it is a general noun + specific noun, which makes a possessive fragment.*

The word هُ *and* رب *cannot be connected because it is specific + general, which is an easy break. We have found our first break.*

رب is connected to السماوات *because it is a general noun + a specific noun, making it a possessive fragment.*

Now let's sort.

دعاء has a receiver label, making the entire fragment (دعاءه) the receiver.

رب has a doer label, making the entire fragment (رب السماوات) the doer.

Note the sequence of the translation is doer -> action -> receiver.

 Go to Chapter 4, Drill #1 - Labelling and Translating Action Sentences.

CONNECTOR LETTERS

As mentioned previously, as long as two words are part of a fragment, they are connected and the boundary continues. In addition to the five fragments, there is one more tool that can connect words to each other. This tool is connector letters. The most common connector in Arabic is و, which translates as "and".

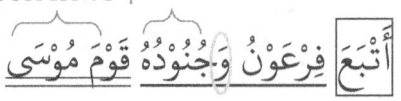

Pharaoh and his army <u>chased</u> the people of Moses.

The word فرعون is connected to جنود because of the connector و.

The ه is connected to جنود because it is general + specific, making it a possessive fragment.

The word هُ and قوم cannot be connected because it is specific + general, which is an easy break. We have found our first break.

We know that قوم موسى are connected because it is a general noun + specfic noun, so it is a possessive fragment.

فرعون has a doer label, therefore the entire fragment is the doer.

قوم has the receiver label, therefore the entire fragment is the receiver.

Note the sequence of the translation is doer -> action -> receiver.

IS SENTENCES

Previously, we studied IS SENTENCES in which there was a single noun on either side of the IS. In reality, any combination of fragments can also appear on either side of the IS.

Our only task, in completing the macro analysis of an IS SENTENCE, is to find the IS. Remember that the IS, in Arabic, is invisible.

To find the IS, simply:

1. Go word by word, looking for relationships between the words

2. <u>**As soon as you find a break in the relationships, you have found your IS.**</u>

3. Place the IS at the first break. In other words, place the IS between the first two words that have no relationship.

Once you have found the IS, complete the micro analysis in order to properly translate the fragments that may appear on either side of the IS.

The Prophet of Allah's home *is* close to the masjid.

بيت رسول الله is general + general + specific, which makes a possessive chain, so all three words are related.

The word الله is specific and the word قريب is general, which makes for an easy break. We have found our first break. This is where we place the "is" in translation.

CONNECTOR LETTERS

As was the case with action sentences, connector letters can appear in *IS SENTENCES*, forming a link between two or more words. A connector letter, in addition to the five fragments, is considered a relationship.

Allah *is* the light of the skies and the earth.

Notice that السموات والأرض is grouped together because of the connector letter between them.

TLDR PHRASES IN SENTENCES

It is quite common for TLDR phrases to appear in both *ACTION* and is sentences. When you see a TLDR phrase, there is no need to do macro analysis of it. Micro analysis is enough.

SHIFTING THE ORDER

The most important thing to know about TLDR phrases in Arabic sentences is that their positioning is more flexible than it is in English sentences. If it sounds awkward to translate a

TLDR phrase according to its actual position in the Arabic, feel free to shift the order in translation.

2:164 ...أَنزَلَ اللّهُ [مِنَ السَّمَاءِ] مَاءً... ﴿١٦٤﴾

Allah sent down [from the sky] water.

Allah sent down water [from the sky].

12:105 ...وَهُم [عَنْهَا] مُعْرِضُونَ ﴿١٠٥﴾

They are [from it] turning away.

They are turning away [from it].

You may have noticed that, in the naturalized version of the translations above, the TLDR phrase is at the end of the sentence. This is the norm in English. TLDR phrases usually go at the end of a sentence.

 Go to Chapter 4, Drill #3A - Shifted TLDR Phrases.

REPHRASING

3:189 وَلِلَّهِ | مُلْكُ السَّمَاوَاتِ وَالْأَرْضِ ... ﴿١٨٩﴾

For Allah is the dominion of the skies and the earth.

Dominion of the skies and the earth belongs to Allah.

There may also be cases in which making a sentence sound natural in translation involves **more** than just moving the TLDR phrase, as in the example above. Though it sounds normal in Arabic to say, "For me is x," that is not how belonging is expressed in English. It is more normal to say, "I have x," or "X belongs to me."

{٦٨} فِيهِمَا | فَاكِهَةٌ وَنَخْلٌ وَرُمَّانٌ   55:68

*In them **are** fruits, date palms, and pomegranates.*

There are fruits, date palms, and pomegranates in them.

Likewise, while it is normal in Arabic to begin a sentence by saying "In it are...," that is not natural in English. This is because TLDR phrases do not usually appear at the beginning of a sentence in English. This structure is more naturally translated as "There are...in it."

☞ *Go to Chapter 4, Drill #3B - Rephrasing.*

ALTERNATIVE TRANSLATIONS FOR TLDR WORDS

{٣}...يُجَادِلُ فِي اللهِ...   22:3

*He argues **about** Allah.*

Naturalizing a sentence may also involve being flexible in your translation of TLDR words. When you studied the TLDR words, you learned one definition for each. In reality, each has multiple meanings. Furthermore, the use of TLDR words differs across languages.

For example, an Arabic speaker would say the equivalent of, "I'm good *in* English," while an English speaker would say, "I'm good *at* Arabic." If فِي is used in such a sentence, and you are translating it to English, you would translate it as "at" rather than "in," because that is what is natural in English.

OMITTING AND INSERTING TLDR WORDS

{١٥٧}...كَذَّبَ بِآيَاتِ اللَّهِ...   6:157

He denied Allah's signs.

$$\{١٦٤\}...وَكَلَّمَ اللهُ مُوسَىٰ...$$ 4:164

*Allah spoke **to** Musa.*

In English, certain actions are associated with certain TLDR words. For example, the action "talked" comes with "to". Other actions are not associated with TLDR words, but come with a receiver instead. For example, you would say, "I saw him," rather than "I saw to/about/from him," because the action "to see" is not associated with a TLDR word.

This is the case in Arabic as well. Certain actions are associated with TLDR words and certain actions come with a receiver. However, there are cases in which the Arabic version of an action comes with a TLDR word, while the English counterpart comes with a receiver. The reverse is also true. There may be cases in which the Arabic action comes with a receiver, while the English counterpart comes with a TLDR word.

Both scenarios are demonstrated in the examples above. In the first example, the word كَذَّبَ comes with the TLDR word ب, but the English equivalent "to deny," comes with a direct receiver. Likewise, the word كَلَّمَ comes with a receiver in Arabic, but the English equivalent "to speak," comes with the word "to."

As always, when translating, translate according to what is natural in English.

☞ *Go to Chapter 4, Drill #3C - Alternative Translations.*

STRINGS OF SENTENCES

Punctuation is not used in classical Arabic, and most ayaat contain more than one sentence within them. We have studied extensively how to dissect and translate complete sentences in isolation. Let us now learn how to find the boundaries of sentences when they appear in strings.

1. ج ط ق م - You will see the following symbols appearing above the text in the standard Uthmani script. These symbols never appear mid-sentence. They always

mark the end of one sentence and the beginning of another. Though these markings do not appear between every sentence, they appear between many and are the simplest and surest way of identifying boundaries.

$$\text{قَالُوا اتَّخَذَ اللَّهُ وَلَدًا ۗ سُبْحَانَهُ ۖ هُوَ الْغَنِيُّ ۖ لَهُ مَا فِي السَّمَاوَاتِ وَمَا فِي الْأَرْضِ ۚ إِنْ عِندَكُم مِّن سُلْطَانٍ بِهَٰذَا ۚ أَتَقُولُونَ عَلَى اللَّهِ مَا لَا تَعْلَمُونَ ﴿٦٨﴾}$$ 10:68

They say, "God has taken a son." | He is above that! | He is the self-sufficient. | Whatever is in the skies and the earth belongs to Him. | You have no authority with regards to this [claim]. | Are you saying about Allah what you do have no knowledge of?

2. و - The connector و usually links two like things (e.g. two nouns or two actions). If you see it linking two different things, it is likely the start of a new sentence. In the example below, the و is linking an action to a TLDR phrase which are two unlike things.

$$\text{هُوَ يُحْيِي وَيُمِيتُ ۖ وَإِلَيْهِ تُرْجَعُونَ ﴿٥٦﴾}$$ 10:56

He gives life and death, and you will be returned to Him.

3. قَال – The action "to say" is always followed by a quote. The quote is starts a new sentence. For example, God said , "I am with you," is two complete sentences. "God said," is a full sentence as it has a DOER and ACTION. The quote "I am with you" is a complete IS SENTENCE containing a BEFORE IS and AFTER IS.

$$\text{... وَقَالَ اللَّهُ إِنِّي مَعَكُمْ ... ﴿١٢﴾}$$ 5:12

And God said, "Certainly, I am with you all."

4. When making a break, always make sure that there is a complete sentence on either side. Sometimes, there is only one viable location for a break.

...مِّنْهُمُ الْمُؤْمِنُونَ | وَأَكْثَرُهُمُ الْفَاسِقُونَ ﴿١١٠﴾ 3:110

*Among them **are** believers, and most of them **are** corrupt.*

ACTION SENTENCES: THE BREAK AND SORT METHOD.

1. The action always comes first. Box it off.
2. Go word by word and check if the words are connected by means of any of the five fragments or a connector letter. If the two words are not connected, place a break.
    a. Remember our list of easy breaks!
    b. Do this for the entire sentence
3. Once you have placed your breaks, check the label on the first word of each fragment chain. The doer will be marked by a doer label and a receiver will be marked by a receiver label.
4. Translate: doer -> action -> receiver -> TLDR phrase

IS SENTENCES:

Find all of the fragment breaks. Remember our list of easy breaks!
Place the "is" at the first break.

TLDR PHRASES:

- Does not play the role of doer or receiver in *ACTION SENTENCES*, it is just extra information
- Can appear in either *ACTION SENTENCES* or *IS SENTENCES*
- When translating, you may have to naturalize the translation by:
    o Shifting the position of the TLDR phrase
    o Rephrasing the sentence (particularly with sentences denoting belonging)
    o Giving the TLDR word a translation other than its standard translation
    o Omitting or adding in a TLDR word in translation

STRINGS OF SENTENCE:

Classically, Arabic does not use punctuation, so to determine where a sentence starts or ends:

- Use the markings above the text in the mushaf (ࣤ ࣫ ࣢ ࣡)
- A connector letter (و) between two unlike things (i.e., a noun + action, or noun + TLDR)
- After قال
- Two complete sentences on either side of the break

CHAPTER 05
ACTIONS: THE MISSING ELEMENT

INTRODUCTION

The core of Arabic is made up of two sentences and five fragments. We have learned almost everything there is to know about these basic structures. There is, however, one key element that we have yet to look at in detail, and that is the action.

As you already know, the action, or the verb, is the first element in an *ACTION SENTENCE*.

Verbs in Arabic conjugate. This means that they change form depending on who is carrying out the action. This is also the case in many other languages, including English. You would say, for example, "I eat." You would not, however, say "She eat". Rather, you would say "She eats". This change in the form of the verb is known as conjugation.

There are twelve pronouns in Arabic. This means that there are twleve different forms an action can take.

We will be studying both past and present tense. You will be introduced to all twelve forms of the past tense action, but the most common forms will be highlighted. Once we have studied how the action conjugates, we will make some observations on how they behave in a sentence.

PAST TENSE - THE FORMS

When a past tense action conjugates, the base of the word will always remain the same. The changes appear only on the end of the action. We will call these endings *INDICATORS*, because they indicate the doer coded into the action.

Remember that actions conjugate according to who the doer of the action is.

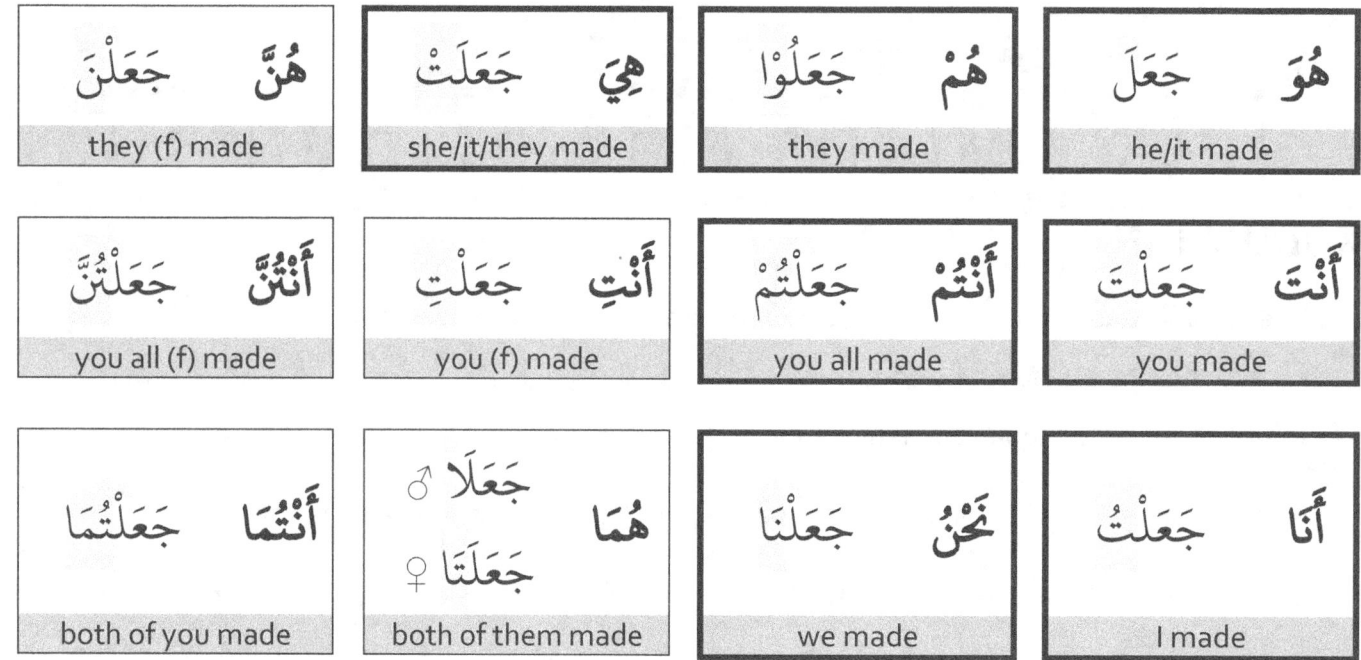

It is important that you have a basic level of familiarity with all twelve forms. In terms of memorization, however, you may focus your energy on the seven forms that have bold borders.

☞ *Go to Chapter 5, Drill #1 - Past Tense Forms and complete Drills 1A + 1B.*

PAST TENSE + PRONOUNS

- Notice that the هم version ends in a ا. This ا is not pronounced and disappears when a pronoun is attached. For example, جَعَلُوا becomes جَعَلُوهُم.

  كَذَّبُوا + هُ = كَذَّبُوهُ   جَاءُوا + نَا = جَاءُونَا   جَعَلُوا + هُم = جَعَلُوهُم

- When a pronoun is attached to the أنتم version, you will find that a و is inserted in between the verb and the attached pronoun. For example, rather than saying جَعَلْتُمْهُ, the word would read جَعَلْتُمُوهُ. This is done to make the word sound smoother and to make it easier to pronounce.

  هَدَيْتُمْ + هَا = هَدَيْتُمُوهَا   سَأَلْتُمْ + نَا = سَأَلْتُمُونَا   جَعَلْتُمْ + هُ = جَعَلْتُمُوهُ

- Notice that the indicator for the "نحن" version is نا. Remember that the attached version of نحن is also نا. To differentiate between the indicator and the attached version, simply look at the letter before the نا:

    o If the letter before the نا has a ْ, it is an indicator

        - جَعَلْنَا – we made

    o If the letter before the نا has any other mark, it is an attached pronoun

        - جَعَلَنَا – he made us

☞ *Go to Chapter 5, Drill 1C – Past Tense + Pronouns.*

PRESENT/FUTURE TENSE - THE FORMS

In Arabic, the same form is used for present and future tense. When a present/future tense action conjugates, the base of the word always remains the same. The changes appear only on the beginning and the ending of the action. We will call these beginnings and endings *INDICATORS*, because they indicate the doer coded into the action. Note the difference between past and present/future. When it comes to <u>*past, the indicators appear only on the end*</u>. When it comes to <u>*present/future, the indicators appear both on the beginning and end*</u>.

Remember that actions conjugate according to who the doer of the action is.

It is important that you have a basic level of familiarity with all twelve forms. In terms of memorization, however, you may focus your energy on the seven forms that have bold borders.

Notice that all present tense actions begin with one of the following letters أ ي ت ن. The beginning + ending is what tells you what pronoun is embedded in the action.

PRONOUN	ENDING	BEGINNING
هُوَ he/it	ُ	يـ
هُمَا both of them	ـانِ	
هُمْ they	وْنَ	
هُنَّ they (f)	ْنَ	
هِيَ أَنْتَ she/it/they you	ُ	تـ
أَنْتُمَا both of you	ـانِ	
أَنْتُمْ you all	وْنَ	
أَنْتِ you (f)	ْيَنَ	
أَنْتُنَّ you all (f)	ْنَ	
أَنَا I	ُ	أ
نَحْنُ we	ُ	نـ

 Go to Chapter 5, Drill #2 - Present Tense Forms.

QUICK CLUES

Although the past and present charts are unique, and each form within each of the two charts is different from the next, there are a few quick clues you can use to quickly identify some of the common forms.

CLUES THAT APPLY TO BOTH PAST AND PRESENT

1. و indicates plural   جَعَلُوْا   يَجْعَلُوْنَ   تَجْعَلُوْنَ
2. ا indicates pair   جَعَلَا   يَجْعَلَانِ   تَجْعَلَانِ
3. نَ indicates feminine   جَعَلْنَ   يَجْعَلْنَ   تَجْعَلْنَ

CLUES THAT APPLY TO PAST ONLY

✓ The second person pronouns (talking *to* someone), the endings on the actions rhyme with their corresponding pronouns.

أَنْتَ جَعَلْتَ	أَنْتُمْ جَعَلْتُمْ	أَنْتِ جَعَلْتِ	أَنْتُنَّ جَعَلْتُنَّ	أَنْتُمَا جَعَلْتُمَا
you made	you all made	you (f) made	you all (f) made	both of you made

CLUES THAT APPLY TO PRESENT ONLY

✓ يَ beginning in present tense indicates the third person (talking *about* someone)

هُوَ يَجْعَلُ	هُمْ يَجْعَلُوْنَ	هُنَّ يَجْعَلْنَ	هُمَا يَجْعَلَانِ
he/it makes	they make	they (f) make	both of them make

✓ If it ends in a ُ it is present/future tense

هُوَ يَجْعَلُ	هِيَ تَجْعَلُ	أَنْتَ تَجْعَلُ	أَنَا أَجْعَلُ	نَحْنُ نَجْعَلُ
he/it makes	she/it/they make	you make	I make	we make

DISTINGUISHING BETWEEN PAST AND PRESENT

Though we learned our past chart and our present/future chart separtely, when reading Quran, the different types of actions will not be sorted for you. This makes it important to differentiate between past and present/future when they appear mixed in a real context. Use the following tips to help you:

1) **_Always start by checking the ending_**. There is NO overlap between past and present/future endings. This means that:

    a. If you see a past tense ending, it is a past tense and your job is done

2) If you see a present tense ending, check the beginning of the word to make sure that it has a present tense beginning as well.

    a. If it has a present/future beginning as well, it is a present/future action.

    b. If it does not, it is not an action. It is a noun.

 Go to Chapter 5, Drill #3 - Past vs Present.

DISTINGUISHING BETWEEN NOUNS AND ACTIONS

Remember that the only thing that distinguishes an ACTION SENTENCE from an IS SENTENCE is that ACTION SENTENCES begin with an action. Therefore, it is very important to be able to recognize an action when you see one. Use the following tips to help you distinguish between actions and nouns.

NOUNS/DESCRIPTIONS

- An action can never have a double accent (ٍ ٌ ً). So if you see a word with a double accent, it is a noun

- If a word has an ال (the), it is a noun. If you think about it logically, it is not possible to add "the" before an action (eg. the walked)

- Remember that a TLDR phrase is a relationship between a TLDR word and a noun. Therefore, if a word comes after a TLDR word, it is a noun

- Remember that a sentence starter fragment is a relationship between a sentence starter and a noun. Therefore, if a word comes after a sentence starter, it is a noun.

- Only a noun can get a ة, so if a word has a ة, it is a noun

ACTIONS

- Past tense ending indicators are unique to actions. So if a word has a past tense indicator, it is definitely a past tense action. Remember, the past indicators are:

- If you see **both** beginning and ending present tense indicators, it is present tense. ***If you have only the beginning or only the ending, then it is NOT a present tense action. You must have both for it to be a present tense action. Otherwise, it is a noun.*** For example, مُخْتَلِفُوْنَ has the ending (وْنَ) but not the beginning, so it is not an action. It is a noun.

Go to Chapter 5, Drill #4 – Distinguishing Between Nouns and Actions

DIFFERENT FORMS IN ACTION SENTENCES

Action forms do not change what we have already learned about the structure of ACTION SENTENCES. An ACTION SENTENCE is still made up of an action, a doer, and a receiver. When a action changes its form, however, the doer is simply encoded into the action. The indicators tell you who the doer is.

When an action has a doer encoded into it, there is no need to search for a noun that has one of the doer labels. When the doer is a pronoun, we can call it an EMBEDDED DOER, because it is embedded in the action.

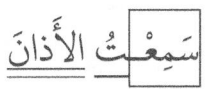

I heard the call to prayer.

Notice that there is no noun that has a doer label in the sentence. This is because the doer is already encoded into the action.

 Go to Chapter 5, Drill #5 — Now in Sentences.

WHAT IF THE DOER IS NOT A PRONOUN?

If the doer is an ordinary noun (e.g. Muhammad, Ayesha etc.) and not a pronoun (e.g. we, she, they etc.), the sentence will follow the format you were taught in the previous chapters. The doer will be an ordinary noun that takes one of the doer labels. We can call this kind of doer an *OUTSIDE DOER*, because it is outside of the action (unlike embedded doers).

Though we have already dealt with this type of sentence extensively, there is one additional observation to be made in light of our knowledge of the different forms.

When a sentence has an outside doer, the actions only ever conjugate in the singular form (هو form or the هي form).

- The هو form is used when the outside doer is male.
- The هي form is used when the outside doer is female.

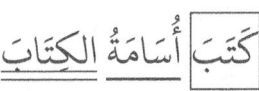

Usama wrote the book.

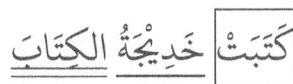

Khadija wrote the book.

Notice that the هي version ends in a ْ . When this word is followed by an ال, you end up with two ْ in a row – the ْ on the end of the first word and the ْ on the beginning of the second word. This arrangement is considered "unpronounceable" because it is difficult to pronounce two stops in a row. For this reason, whenever followed by an ال, the ْ on the action changes to a ِ to facilitate flow pronunciation.

قَالَتْ ٱلْأَعْرَابُ   قَالَتِ ٱلْأَعْرَابُ

Actions change form **ACCORDING TO WHO THE DOER** is

- When the **DOER** is a **PRONOUN**:

    o It is **EMBEDDED IN THE ACTION** itself

    o An **INDICATOR** on the action will tell you what the embedded doer is

    ▪ For **PAST TENSE ACTIONS**, the indicator will be at the **END**. For **PRESENT TENSE ACTIONS**, there will be indicators at the **BEGINNING AND THE END**

    ▪ There will be no outside doer if the doer is already embedded

- When the **DOER** is a **NORMAL NOUN**

    o Will come **AFTER THE ACTION** and have one of the **DOER LABELS** (ـٌ / ـٍ انِ وْنَ اتٌ / اتُ)

    o The action will be in the هو **FORM** if the outside **DOER IS MALE**

    o The action will be in the هي **FORM** if the outside **DOER IS FEMALE**

DISTINGUISHING BETWEEN NOUNS AND ACTIONS:

NOUNS/DESCRIPTIONS	ACTION
-double accent (ـٌ ـٍ)	-past tense ending indicators (i.e., ـَتْ ـْتُ ـْتُمْ ـْنَا)
-ال	-present tense beginning and ending indicators (i.e., تَـ + يْنَ ,يَـ + وْنَ ,أَ + ـُ , etc.)
-comes after a TLDR word	
-comes after a sentence starter	
-ةـ	

OUR TERM	FORMAL TERM	ARABIC TERM
past tense action	past tense verb	فِعْل مَاض
present tense action	present tense verb	فِعْل مُضَارِع
forms	conjugation	تَصْرِيْف
male	masculine	مُذَكَّر
female	feminine	مُؤَنَّث
embedded doer/indicator	subject pronoun	ضَمِيْر مُتَّصِل/فَاعِل مُتَّصِل
outside doer	subject	فَاعِل صَرِيْح
singular	"	مُفْرَد
pair	"	مُثَنَّى
plural	"	جَمْع
first person	"	مُتَكَلِّم
second person	"	مُخَاطَب
third person	"	غَائِب

CHAPTER 06
THE ANOMALIES

INTRODUCTION

Every language has its irregularities, and Arabic is no exception. The rules we learned over the past five chapters are the standard. They apply most of the time. There are cases, however, in which these rules change slightly.

We will be dividing this study into three categories:

1. exceptions that occur on a **_sentence level_**
2. exceptions that occur on a **_word level_**
3. exceptions that occur on a **_fragment level_**

These three categories are arranged in order of priority, based on which exceptions occur most frequently.

SENTENCE LEVEL ANOMALIES

Exceptions that occur on a sentence level occur both in *ACTION SENTENCES* and *IS SENTENCES*. We will explore these exceptions in that order, starting with the two exceptions that occur in *ACTION SENTENCES*, followed by the two exceptions that occur in *IS SENTENCES*.

ACTION SENTENCE ANOMALIES

ACTION SENTENCE ANOMALY #1 - DOER BEFORE ACTION

We learned that, in an *ACTION SENTENCE*, the action always comes first. The doer and receiver can then follow in any order.

Though it is not the grammatical standard, it is possible for the doer to come before the action. This is done for rhetorical purposes. The doer is brought before the action to give special attention to the doer. The purpose of giving extra emphasis to the doer is highlighting that it was the doer, and not anyone else, who carried the action out.

Though this breaks standard *grammatical* convention, it is used quite commonly in the Quran.

⟨٤٥⟩...﴾مِنْ مَاءٍ﴿ خَلَقَ كُلَّ دَابَّةٍ وَاللَّهُ   24:45

Allah created every creature [from water].

⟨٣١⟩...﴾عَلَىٰ ظُهُورِهِمْ﴿ يَحْمِلُونَ أَوْزَارَهُمْ وَهُمْ...   6:31

...and they will be carrying their burdens [on their backs].

⟨٢٦⟩...﴾عَنْ نَفْسِي﴿ رَاوَدَتْنِي هِيَ...   12:26

She tried to seduce me [against my will].

⟨٥١⟩...﴾عَنْ نَفْسِهِ﴿ رَاوَدْتُهُ أَنَا...   12:51

I tried to seduce him [against his will].

If a sentence starter and its noun come before an action, the entire fragment will act as the doer.

⟨٥٦⟩...﴾عَلَى النَّبِيِّ﴿ يُصَلُّونَ إِنَّ اللَّهَ وَمَلَائِكَتَهُ   33:56

Certainly, God and His angels send salutations [to the Prophet].

☞ *Go to Chapter 6, Drill #1A - The Doer's New Position.*

ACTION SENTENCE ANOMALY #2 - RECEIVER BEFORE ACTION

We learned that, in an *ACTION SENTENCE*, the action always comes first. The doer and receiver can then follow in any order.

It is possible for the receiver to come before the action, though it is not the grammatical standard. However, unlike the previous anomaly, this does not happen often. This is done for rhetorical purposes. The receiver is brought forward to show exclusivity. In translation, the exclusivity is captured by including the word "alone" or "only." It is recognized by a noun with a receiver label coming before the action.

39:14 ... اللَّهَ أَعْبُدُ ... ﴿١٤﴾

"I worship Allah alone..."

Recall that any pronoun that attaches to an action is a receiver. It is also possible for this type of receiver to be brought forward to show exclusivity. However, attached pronouns must always have something to attach to. For this reason, when a receiver pronoun is brought forward, the placeholder إِيَّا is used as a "chair" for the pronoun to sit on.

1:5 إِيَّاكَ نَعْبُدُ / وَإِيَّاكَ نَسْتَعِينُ ﴿٥﴾

We worship You alone and we rely on You alone.

Though the receiver coming before the action is not rare, it is not happen as frequently as the doer coming before the action.

☞ *Go to Chapter 6, Drill #1B - The Receiver's New Position.*

IS SENTENCE ANOMALIES

Recall that the *IS* in Arabic is invisible. To find it, you simply search for the first break in relationships between words. While this is the standard rule, there are two cases in which the *IS* does not go at the first break.

IS SENTENCE ANOMALY #1: "IS SENTENCE" EMPHASIZERS

We saw in the previous section that, in an *ACTION SENTENCE*, the doer can be emphasized. Similarly, in an *IS SENTENCE*, the *BEFORE IS* can also be emphasized.

The *BEFORE IS* can be highlighted using what we call *EMPHASIZER PRONOUNS*. An emphasizer pronoun is a pronoun added directly after the *BEFORE IS*. This structure is easy to spot, because independent pronouns generally appear as the first element in an *IS SENTENCE*, so if you see an independent pronoun in the middle of an *IS SENTENCE*, it is an emphasizer pronoun.

42:9 ﴿٩﴾ ... وَاللهُ هُوَ | الوَلِيُّ ...

Allah, HE *is* the true ally.

29:64 ﴿٦٤﴾ ... وَإِنَّ الدَّارَ الآخِرَةَ لَهِيَ | الحَيَوانُ ...

Certainly, the afterlife, IT *is* the true life.

Notice that the *IS* goes **_after_** the pronoun in both examples.

Though it seems like the break occurs before the pronoun, the pronoun here is a filler used to add emphasis and highlight the topic.

For this reason, it would not make sense for the *IS* to go before the pronoun (i.e., Allah is He the true ally).

Also note that translating the pronoun literally (as done in the examples above) may sound natural in speech, but unusual in writing. A more formal alternative would be to capture the emphasis on the topic by using the "It is x who/that..." template. For example, "It is Allah who is the true ally," or "It is the afterlife that is the true life."

 Go to Chapter 6, Drill #2A - Emphasizer Pronouns.

IS SENTENCE ANOMALY #2: SENTENCE STARTER INTERRUPTERS

Consider the following sentence:

... فِيهَا | لُوطًا ... ﴿٣٢﴾   29:32

*In it **is** Lut*

*Lut **is** in it*

The sentence above is a standard *IS SENTENCE*. There is a break between فِيهَا and لُوطًا, so that is where the *IS* goes. The translation can then be naturalized by moving the TLDR phrase to the end.

Now consider the following sentence:

... إِنَّ | فِيهَا | لُوطًا ... ﴿٣٢﴾   29:32

*...Certainly, in it **is** Lut...*

*...Certainly, Lut **is** in it...*

This sentence is the same as the previous sentence with one difference: it begins with the sentence starter word إِنَّ, which is added to emphasize the sentence. Notice that, although there is a break between إِنَّ and فِيهَا, it would not make sense for the *IS* to go there (certainly is in it Lut). This is because **when a sentence starter is followed directly by a TLDR phrase, the "is" goes after the TLDR phrase, NOT before.** This is the second case in which the *IS* does not go at the first break.

 Go to Chapter 6, Drill #2B - Sentence Starter Anomalies.

WORD LEVEL ANOMALY - WORDS THAT DO NOT TAKE LABELS

There are certain words that do no accept labels. This occurs with both nouns and actions. There are specific types of nouns that do not take labels. There are also specific types of actions that do not take indicators. We will start with nouns, then look at actions.

NOUNS THAT DO NOT TAKE LABELS

Recall that, in an *ACTION SENTENCE*, the doer and receiver are determined based on the labels. There are two sets of labels that we learned. As mentioned earlier, there are some words that do not like to accept labels. The endings of these words do not change, regardless of the role they are playing in a sentence.

There are four categories of words that do not accept labels, two of which we are already familiar with. They are:

1. Pronouns

2. Pointers

3. Words that end in ى or ا

4. Words that have the pronoun ي attached to them

Note that the attached pronoun ي erases the label of the word that it attaches to, even if that word would normally accept a label. For example, كِتَابٌ becomes كِتَابِي, causing the label to disappear. This is done to make pronunciation of the word smoother.

 Go to Chapter 6, Drill #3A - Labels or No?.

Remember that labels are the means by which we are able to identify the doer and receiver in an *ACTION SENTENCE*. If the doer or receiver happen to be a word that does not accept labels, we will have to identify them through other means. We will use a combination of clues and common sense to accomplish this.

1. It is not often that both the doer and receiver are words that do not accept a label. If you are able to identify one, you have identified the other.

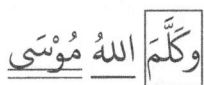

Allah spoke to Musa.

The word الله has a doer label. This means that موسى must be the receiver.

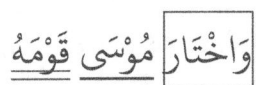

Musa chose his people.

The word قوم has a receiver label. This means that موسى must be the doer.

2. If the doer is embedded, there cannot be an outside doer. This means that the label-less word must be the receiver.

وَوَاعَدْنَا مُوسَى أَرْبَعِينَ لَيْلَةً

We promised Musa forty days.

The action has the embedded doer نحن. This means that the doer slot is taken, which means that موسى must be the receiver.

3. Pay attention to the meaning and use common sense

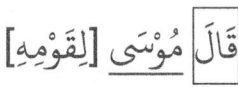

Musa said [to his people]...

If موسى was labelled as a receiver, the sentence would translate as "He said 'Musa' to his people," which is unlikely, in general, and does not make sense in the context of the ayah.

 Go to Chapter 6, Drill #3B - Role of Label-less Words.

ACTIONS THAT DO NOT TAKE INDICATORS

Recall that, in the past tense, the ending indicators tell us what embedded pronoun is within. In the present tense, the ending and beginning indicators tell us what embedded doer is within. There is one scenario in which actions do not take indicators. **Actions ending in a vowel (ا و ي) do not accept certain indicators.** Luckily, this only happens in a handful of forms.

INDICATOR-LESS ACTIONS IN THE PAST TENSE

In a past-tense ending in a vowel, only the هو form does not accept its regular indicator. Look at the table below. Notice that the only form missing the indicator is the هو form.

INDICATOR-LESS ACTIONS IN THE PRESENT TENSE

In the present-tense, only the forms normally ending in ُ do not accept their regular indicators. The forms that end in ُ are: نحن, أنا, أنتَ, هي, هو. Notice that these are the only forms that are missing the indicator. The remaining forms look the same.

Though these forms no longer have their normal endings, you can still recognized the embedded doer by the beginnings.

FRAGMENT LEVEL ANOMALIES

FRAGMENT LEVEL ANOMALY #1: POINTING AT POSSESSIVES

When we studied fragment chains, we saw that fragments can come together in all sorts of different orders. One of the most unique fragment combinations is the pointer+possessive combination, or when you are pointing at a possessive fragment.

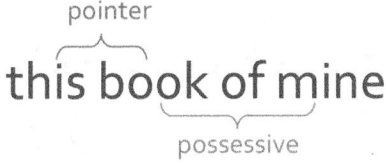

"Book of mine" is a possessive fragment. It is being pointed at using the word "this".

The Arabic version of this fragment combination is unique in that the pointer comes <u>*after*</u> the things that is being pointed at. This is only the case when you are pointing at a possessive fragment. In any other case, the pointer comes first.

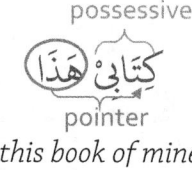

this book of mine

This fragment combination is not all that common, so the easiest way to recognize it is to learn all the cases in which this fragment combination occurs.

21:63 كَبِيرُهُمْ هَذَا *this leader of theirs*	25:17 عِبَادِىْ هَؤُلَاءِ *these servants of Mine*	12:15 بِأَمْرِهِمْ هَذَا *about this matter of theirs*
18:19 بِوَرِقِكُمْ هَذِهِ *this money of yours*	12:93 بِقَمِيْصِىْ هَذَا *with this shirt of mine*	27:28 بِكِتَابِىْ هَذَا *with this book of mine*
	9:27 بَعْدَ عَامِهِمْ هَذَا *after this year of theirs*	

☞ *Go to Chapter 6, Drill #5: Pointing at Possessives.*

FRAGMENT LEVEL ANOMALY #2: PAIR + PLURAL ITEM

Recall that pair and plural words are marked by the following endings: وْنَ، ِيْنَ، ان، َيْنِ. Notice that the one thing these endings all have in common is that the last letter is a ن.

When a pair or plural word is the item (in a possessive fragment), the ن disappears.

أَبَوَاهُ

his (two) parents

The pair form of أَب is أَبَوَان. Since أَبَوَان is acting as the item, the ن drops, leaving us with أَبَوا

مُهْلِكُو أَهْلِ هَذِهِ الْقَرْيَةِ

the destroyers of the people of this town

The plural form of مُهْلِك is مُهْلِكُونَ. Since مُهْلِكُونَ is acting as the item, the ن drops, leaving us with مُهْلِكُو

If you see a item ending in و، ا، ي it is possible that it is a dual or plural that has lost its ن.

 Go to Chapter 6, Drill #6: Dual/Plural Possessed.

ACTION SENTENCES ANOMALIES

- *Doer before action:* is a noun with a doer label coming before the action. Done to highlight to doer. A sentence starter and its noun before an action will also be the doer.

- *Receiver before action*: is a noun with a receiver lable coming before the action. If it is a pronoun, it will have to sit on the إِيَّ chair. Produces the meaning "only".

IS SENTENCES ANOMALIES

- *Emphasizer pronouns:* are independent pronouns that come in the middle of an action sentence. The IS will go **_after_** the emphasizer pronoun.

- *Sentence Starter Interrupters*: a TLDR phrase can come right after a sentence starter. The IS will go **_after_** the TLDR phrase.

WORD LEVEL ANOMALIES

- *Label resistant words*: are words that cannot show their label. They are words that end in ى/ا, ي, pronouns, and pointers.

- *Indicator-less actions*: actions that end in a vowel (ا/و/ي) will sometimes be missing their ending indicator. In the past tense, it affects the هو form. In the present tense, it affects any action that originally ended in ـُ, so نحن أنَا أنتَ هو هي.

FRAGMENT LEVEL

- *Pointing at possessive*: when pointing at a possessive fragment in Arabic, the **_pointer goes at the end_** of the fragment

- *Pair/plural item*: when something pair or plural is acting as the item in a possessive fragment, the ن will be dropped, leaving behind a ا/و/ي.

OUR TERM	FORMAL TERM	ARABIC TERM
doer before action	subject	مُبْتَدَأ[1]
receiver before action	-	مَفْعُوْل بِهِ مُقَدَّم
emphasizer pronoun	-	ضَمِيْر الفَصْلِ
sentence starter interrupted	-	مُبْتَدَأ مُؤَخَّر
label resistant words	-	مَبْنِيّ

[1] when a doer comes before the action, the sentence is technically considered a nominal sentence (is sentence) with a verbal sentence (action sentence) acting as a predicate

CHAPTER 07
THE PASSIVE VOICE

INTRODUCTION

Remember that the core parts of an *ACTION SENTENCE* are the action and the doer. Without these two parts, the action sentence is not complete. There is one special case, however, in which an *ACTION SENTENCE* does not have a doer. This special case is the use of the passive voice.

The passive voice is a construction in which the doer is omitted. The sentence, "My bike was stolen," is an example of the passive voice. This sentence tells us what happened, but does not specify who made it happen. In other words, the doer is not specified.

Our study of the passive voice will involve:

1. Studying the sentence structure of a sentence containing a passive
2. Studying the patterns of a passive action on a word-level

☞ *Go to Chapter 7 , Drill #1A - Passive or Active?.*

SENTENCE STRUCTURE

Since a passive sentence does not have a doer, how do we label it? A passive sentence is made up of two core components. They are:

1. The passive action
2. The substitute doer

My bike was stolen.

Notice that the word that has been labeled as a "substitute doer" (my bike) is sitting in the doer's seat. It translates first, just like a normal doer.

Go to Chapter 7, Drill #1B - Sentence Structure.

The substitute doer is similar to the doer in two ways:

1. it sits in the doer's seat, meaning it will translate first
2. it takes a doer label

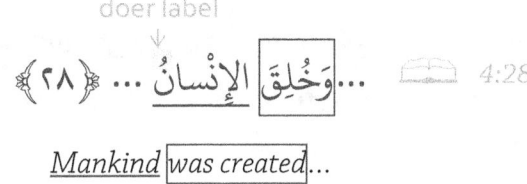

4:28

...وَخُلِقَ الْإِنْسَانُ ... ﴿٢٨﴾

Mankind was created...

The word الإنسان looks like a doer based on the label it carried. It translates first in the English, just like a normal doer.

EMBEDDED AND OUTSIDE SUBSTITUTE DOERS

Recall that there are two types of doers: embedded and outside. Remember, also, that a substitute doer behaves like a doer. This means that a substitute doer also has two forms: embedded and outside.

Just like a normal outside doer, the outside substitute doer will have one of the following labels:

اتٌ / اتُ	ـُونَ	ـانِ	ـَ / ـُ
PLURAL (WOMEN/INANIMATE OBJECTS)	**PLURAL**	**PAIR**	**STANDARD**

Also like a normal outside doer, the action can only be in the هو or هي form when there is an outside substitute doer.

To learn about embedded substitute doers, let us study the passive verb forms.

PASSIVE FORMS

Recall that an embedded doer can be identified based on indicators on the action. In the past-tense, the indicators appear at the end of the action. In the present/future-tense, the indicators appear to the beginning and end of the action. This is also the case with passive actions. As a matter of fact, <u>**the indicators that appear on a normal action and the indicators that appear on a passive action are identical. The only difference between normal actions and passive actions is the vowel marking (حَرَكات) on the body of the action.**</u> These changes in vowel markings vary from past to present/future, so we will study each separately.

*   *   *

PAST PASSIVE

As mentioned previously, past passives have the same ending indicators as normal past-tense actions. The only thing that distinguishes them is the vowel markings on the body of the action. **<u>Past passives are recognizable based on the ُ on the first letter and the ِ on the second-to-last letter.</u>**

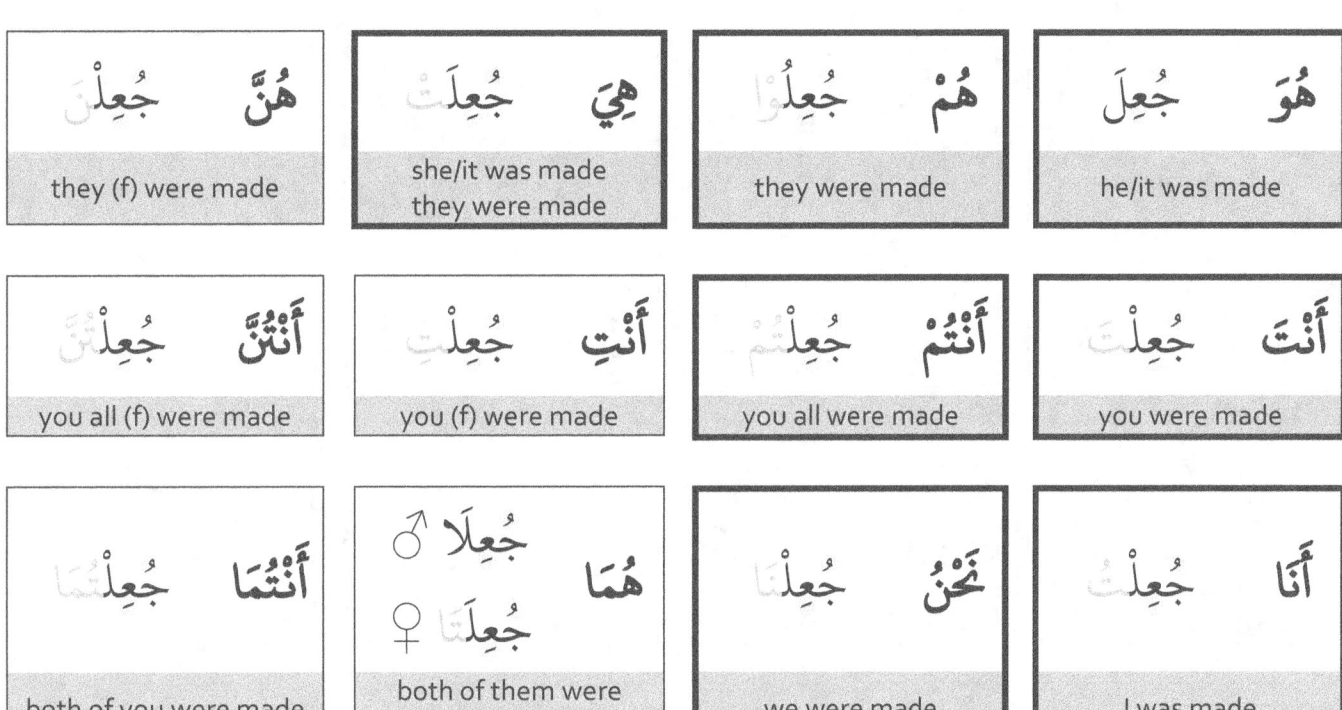

Note that the indicators on the end are not considered a part of the actual action. This means that when looking for the ِ on the second-to-last letter, you should ignore the indicators.

☞ *Go to Chapter 7, Drill #2 - Past Passives.*

PRESENT PASSIVE

As mentioned previously, present passives have the same beginning and ending indicators as normal present-tense action. The only thing that distinguishes them is the vowel markings on the body of the action. **_Present passives are recognizable based on the ؙ on the first letter and the ؘ on the second-to-last letter._**

 they (f) are made	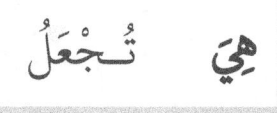 she/it is made / they are made	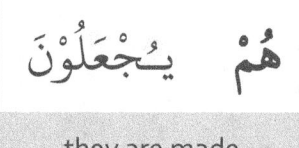 they are made	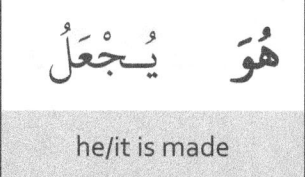 he/it is made
 you all (f) are made	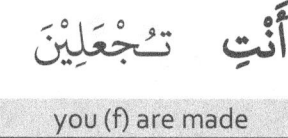 you (f) are made	 you all are made	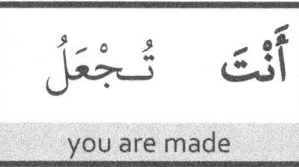 you are made
أَنْتُمَا تُجْعَلَانِ both of you are made	هُمَا يُجْعَلَانِ both of them are made	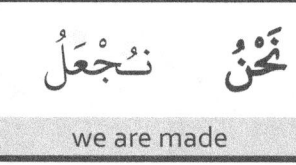 we are made	 I am made

Note that the indicators on the end are not considered a part of the actual action. This means that when looking for the ؘ on the second-to-last letter, you should ignore the indicators.

 Go to Chapter 7, Drill #3 - Present Passives.

Remember that the u-i pattern tells you that a word is passive only when the action is in the past tense. The u-i pattern on a present tense does NOT make a word passive. There are some present tense actions follow the u-i pattern and they are NOT passive.

يُعَلِّمُ = he teaches   يُجَادِلُ = he argues   يُشْرِكُ = he associates partners

Remember to check the tense of the action before trying to figure out whether it is active or passive.

 Go to Chapter 7, Drill #4: Mixed Practice.

PUTTING IT ALL TOGETHER

Once you have identified that an action is passive and you have identified the substitute doer, translation is easy. Simply:

1. Translate the substitute doer first (as you do with a normal doer)

2. Translate the action

    i. Past passives translate as: *[doer] was [action]ed*

    ii. Present passives translate as: *[doer] is [action]ed*

2. Translate all other elements in the sentence, if there are any

 Go to Chapter 7, Drill #5: Now in Sentences.

Passive voice used when doer isn't mentioned or known. Substitute doers sit in the doer's seat and take a doer label.

PAST PASSIVES

- marked by the **U-I PATTERN** (ُ on the first letter, ي/ِ on the second to last letter)

- translates as: [doer] **was** [action]ed.

PRESENT PASSIVES

- marked by the **U-A PATTERN** (ُ on the first letter, ا/َ on the second to last letter)

- translates as: [doer] **is** [action]ed.

OUR TERM	FORMAL TERM	ARABIC TERM
past passive	"	فِعْل مَاض مَبْنِيّ لِلْمَجْهُوْلِ
present passive	"	فِعْل مُضَارِع مَبْنِيّ لِلْمَجْهُوْلِ
substitute doer	subject of predicate	نَائِب الفَاعِلِ

MODULE 1: CORE STRUCTURES

IS SENTENCES

BEFORE IS
usually specific

AFTER IS
usually general

- is invisible in Arabic
- occurs when at the first fragment break

is placement
- in the case of an emphasizer pronoun, the *is* will go after the emphasizer pronoun
- in the case that a TLDR phrase comes right after sent. starter, the *is* will go after the TLDR phrase

---

ACTION SENTENCES

① THE ACTION

past tense: recognized by ending indicators
present tense: recognized by
  beginnings: أ، ن، ي، ت   endings: ـَ، ـْ، ـِ، ـُ، ـَةُ

past passive: ـُ on first letter and ـِ on second to last
present passive: ـُ on the first letter, ـَ/ـَ on second to last

*** passive actions have the same indicators as normal actions

② THE DOER

two types

EMBEDDED
- conjugated within action
- recognized by indicators

OUTSIDE
- comes after the action
- label: فَاعِل، فَا، فَ، فـ

*** passive actions get substitute doers, which follow all the same rules as normal doers, except it will translate as "[subduer] is/was [action]ed".

- only occurs if action is مَـ or يُـ

③ THE RECEIVER

✺ label: مَفْعُول، مَفْ، مَ، مـ/ـ OR a pronoun attached to an action

Use "break and sort" method to label and translate.

ANOMALIES

changes in sequence
normal sequence: ACTION -> DOER -> RECEIVER
- DOER -> ACTION -> RECEIVER
  - a noun with a doer label coming before the action OR a sentence starter and its noun coming before the action
- RECEIVER -> ACTION -> DOER
  - a noun with a receiver label coming before the action
- if the receiver is a pronoun, it will be accompanied by إيّا

- THE FRAGMENTS -

*these roles can be **one word** or **a fragment***
❋ *label-less words may play these roles*

① POSSESSIVE

- noun + noun
- item
  - always the 1st word
  - always general
  - will not have the ال at the end if it is pair or plural
- owner
  - always the 2nd word
  - usually specific
- can come in chains

② DESCRIPTIVE

- noun + adjective
- first word is always the described (noun)
- second word is always the description (adjective)
- both words will always match in generality/specificity
- when describing a possessive fragment (i.e., my black cats), the description will have an ال
- general + general + specific
- the second word will be owner and item at the same time

③ POINTER

- pointer + noun with ال
- *if the word does not have ال, it is not a fragment!
- to point at a possessive, the pointer goes after the possessive fragment

④ SENTENCE STARTERS

- sentence starter + noun
- will come at the start of a sentence

⑤ TLDR PHRASE

- TLDR word + noun
- position is flexible in Arabic, but will usually translate at the end in English
- translation of the TLD is flexible and may vary depending on the word it is related to (if it is translated at all)
- ***does not play a specific role in action sentences

FRAGMENT CHAINS

- two words can be connected by means of the five fragments or a connector letter
- 3 easy ways to identify breaks between words (or easy breaks)
  1. between a specific word and a general word
  2. between two specific nouns
  3. before a TLDR

MODULE
- 2 -

MORE ON ACTIONS

A survey of new varieties of actions as well as new contexts in which actions may appear

CHAPTER 08
BACK-TO-BACK ACTIONS

INTRODUCTION

Typically, an ACTION SENTENCE contains only one action. We previously learned that a new action means a new sentence. Thus far, we have never seen two actions appearing back-to-back in an ACTION SENTENCE. If ever there was a sentence with more than one action, the actions had the connector letter و between them.

47:12 ... ﴿١٢﴾ يَتَمَتَّعُونَ وَيَأْكُلُونَ كَمَا تَأْكُلُ الْأَنْعَامُ ...

They enjoy themselves **and** eat just like cattle do.

There are a few cases, however, in which two actions can appear back-to-back without a connector letter. They are:

1. Saying that something **was** happening or **used to** happen

    I was eating/I used to eat a bag of chips everyday when I was young.

2. Saying that something **almost** happened

    He almost fell off the ladder.

3. Expressing someone/something's **state of being** while performing an action (an adverb)

    He came running from the farthest part of the city.

Let us study each sentence type in more detail.

WAS DOING/USED TO DO

The action كَانَ means "to be." In its past tense form, it translates as "was" and is one action that can appear back-to-back with another action. When كَانَ is followed by a **present tense** action, it produces the meaning "used to do…" or "was doing…"

… كُنتُمْ تُعَلِّمُونَ الْكِتَابَ … ﴿٧٩﴾   3:79

…you all used to teach the book…

كَانَ is in the past tense and the action that follows it directly (تعلمون) is a present tense action. Notice that this combination translates as "used to".

… إِنَّمَا كُنَّا نَخُوضُ وَنَلْعَبُ … ﴿٦٥﴾   9:65

We were only joking and playing.

كَانَ is in the past tense and the actions that follows it directly (نخوض نلعب) are present tense actions. Notice that this combination translates as "was doing".

Just as we have seen with action sentences before, the action can have an embedded doer or an outside doer, as is in the example below.

… كَانَ يَقُولُ سَفِيهُنَا [عَلَى اللَّهِ] شَطَطًا ﴿٤﴾   72:4

The foolish among us used to say lies [against Allah].

… كَانَ آبَاؤُهُمْ لَا يَعْلَمُونَ شَيْئًا … ﴿١٠٤﴾   5:104

Their forefathers did not used to know anything.

When translating, if you are having trouble because it feels like there is a lot going on in the sentence, remember that this structure is a normal ACTION SENTENCE with the addition of a special action, كَانَ, before it. You can always:

1. Hide the special action temporarily

2. Translate the ACTION SENTENCE

3. Re-incorporate the special action by adding "was" or "used to" to the translation

If you are able to translate in a single step, there is no problem with that either.

☞ *Go to Chapter 8, Drill #1: Used to Sentences.*

ALMOST

The word for "almost" in Arabic is كَادَ يَكَادُ. Like the كَانَ, these words are followed by a complete ACTION SENTENCE. Unlike كَانَ, however, the كَادَ can appear in either the past or the present.

… ﴿١٥٠﴾ وَكَادُوا يَقْتُلُونَنِي …   📖 7:150

They almost killed me.

Here, كاد is in the past tense, therefore the action translates in the past tense (almost killed).

… ﴿٨﴾ تَكَادُ تَمَيَّزُ [مِنَ الْغَيْظِ] …   📖 67:8

It almost tears up [with rage].

Here, تكاد is in the present tense, therefore the action translates in the present tense (almost tears).

… ﴿٢٠﴾ يَكَادُ الْبَرْقُ يَخْطَفُ أَبْصَارَهُمْ …   📖 2:20

<u>The lightening</u> |almost| |snatches away| <u>their sight</u>.

Here يكاد is in the present tense, therefore the action translates in the present tense (almost snatches).

The word after كاد/يكاد will translate according to tense of كاد/يكاد, not of the action itself.

Again, you may use the same translation strategy mentioned previously by removing and re-incorporating the "almost."

 Go to Chapter 8 , Drill #2: Almost.

STATE OF BEING

A state of being, also known as an adverb, tells us the state of someone or something as the action is happening. Take a look at the following examples.

The students ran into the classroom [panting].

"Panting" is explaining the state of the students as they ran into the classroom. "Panting" is a state of being, or an adverb.

I kiss my children [while they are sleeping].

"While they are sleeping" is explaining the state of my children when I kiss them. "While they are sleeping" is a state of being, or an adverb.

We listen to that podcast [as we eat breakfast].

"As we eat breakfast" is explaining our state as we listen to podcast. "As we eat breakfast" is a state of being, or an adverb.

In Arabic a state of being appears as a present tense action coming at the end of an ACTION SENTENCE. Note that when we say "the end of a sentence", this does not include TLDRs because their position is flexible.

When you see two actions appearing in the same sentence with no connector letter between them, you're looking at a state of being. The first action describes *what is happening*, the second describes *how it is happening*.

A state of being will usually translate as "-ing", "-ly", "while", or "as".

... ﴿وَجَاءَهُ قَوْمُهُ يُهْرَعُونَ [إِلَيْهِ] ...٧٨﴾   11:78

His people came rushing [to him].

There are two actions in a single sentence (جاء، يهرعون) without a connector letter between them. This tells us that we are looking at a state of being. The action "came" tells us what is happening, and the action "rushing" tells us how it is happening. In other words, it is the state of the nation as they come.

Notice the "-ing" translation of the state of being.

... ﴿وَتَرَاهُمْ يُعْرَضُونَ [عَلَيْهَا] ...٤٥﴾   42:45

You see them being exposed [to it].

There are two actions in a single sentence (ترى، يعرضون) without a connector letter between them. This tells us that we are looking at a state of being. The action "see" tells us what is happening, and the action "being exposed" is their state as you see watch them.

Notice the "-ing" translation of the state of being.

﴿وَجَاءَ رَجُلٌ [مِّنْ أَقْصَى الْمَدِينَةِ] يَسْعَىٰ ...٢٠﴾   28:20

A man came rushing [from the farthest part of the city]...

86

There are two actions in a single sentence (جاء يسعى) without a connector letter between them. This tells us that we are looking at a state of being. The action "came" tells us what is happening, and the action "rushing" how it is happening. In other words, it describes the man's state as he comes.

Notice the "-ing" translation of the state of being.

Note that the "used to" and "almost" structures that we studied earlier involve a specific set of actions (كان، كاد). The state of being structure is also a action+action structure, but it differs in that it does not involve a specific set of actions. Any two actions can be combined in this structure. This is because any action can be done in any state. This can make it easy to miss. Remember, if you see two actions in the same sentence, with no connector between them, it is the state of being structure.

As far as translation and understanding, an important question to ask yourself is: Whose state is being described? This is because most sentence contain multiple people/pronouns. For instance:

1. In the sentence "His people came rushing to him," the word "rushing" describes the state. But whose state is it? Is it "his people" or "him"? In this case, it is his people who are rushing.

2. In the sentence "You see them being exposed to it," the word "being exposed" describes the state. But whose state is it? Is it "you" or "them"? In this case, it is "them."

Figuring out whose state is being described is often a matter of intuition and common sense. If those two things ever fail you, however, there is a grammatical method by which this can be identified. The pronoun in the action that describes the state will match with the one being described. You will notice that this applies in all the examples above.

 Go to Chapter 8 , Drill #3: Adverbs.

THE NOT-SO-ABNORMAL

Of the two special actions that we studied in this chapter, there is one that can appear outside of this structure. The action كان can appear as an ordinary action in ordinary action sentences. As a matter of fact, it is used normally more often than it is used in the action+action structure. كان retains the same meaning (were, was).

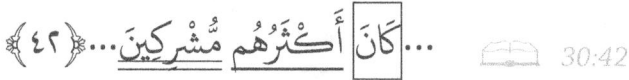

Most of them were polytheists.

كان is followed by an ordinary doer (أكثرهم) and an ordinary receiver (مشركين), and translates in the normal sequence.

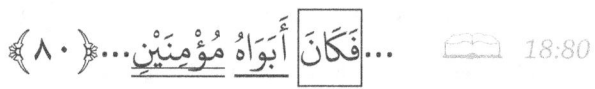

His parents were believers.

كان is followed by an ordinary doer (أبواه) and an ordinary receiver (مؤمنين), and translates in the normal sequence.

☞ Go to Chapter 8, Drill #4: Not-so-Abnormal Action.

☞ Go to Chapter 8, Drill #5: Cummulative Practice.

كانَ + Present Tense

- Translates as "was doing/used to do".

كاد/يكاد + Present Tense

- كاد + present tense action = almost did
- يكاد + present tense action = almost does

State of Being

- State of being tells us the state of someone or something as an action happens
- In Arabic, it will be a present tense action coming at the end of an action sentence with no connector letter between the actions
    - "end of the sentence" does not include TLDRs, as their position is flexible
- Will usually translate to "-ing", "-ly", "while", or "as"

Additional Points

- As with normal ACTION SENTENCES, the doer can come before the action.
- كان can be used normally, outside of the action+action structure. It will simply translate as "was" (if كان is past) or "will be" (if كان is present).

Translation tip: removed special action, translate, re-incorporate

OUR TERM	FORMAL TERM	ARABIC TERM
special action	hollow verb	فِعْل نَاقِص
state of being	adverb	حَال

CHAPTER 09
BALD ACTIONS

CHANGES IN ACTION ENDINGS

Past tense action endings **_never change_**. Present tense action endings, on the other hand, are subject to change. Remember that the present tense action endings (along with the beginnings) tell us about the embedded pronoun within. When the endings change, so do the indicators that tell us about the embedded pronouns. For this reason, it is important to learn about any changes that occur within the endings. Learning these changes will help you correctly identify embedded pronouns.

WHEN DO THESE CHANGES OCCUR?

These changes to present tense action endings do not just happen at random. There are a few specific situations in which present tense action endings are affected. Over the next five chapters, we will be studying the different situations in which present tense endings are affected.

WHAT DO THESE CHANGES LOOK LIKE?

While there are five different scenarios in which present tense endings go through a change, the good news it that **_the change is always the same_**. As stated previously, over the next five chapters, we will be studying the different situations in which these changes occur. Since these changes are always the same, however, we will take the time now to study these change and to put a name to this concept.

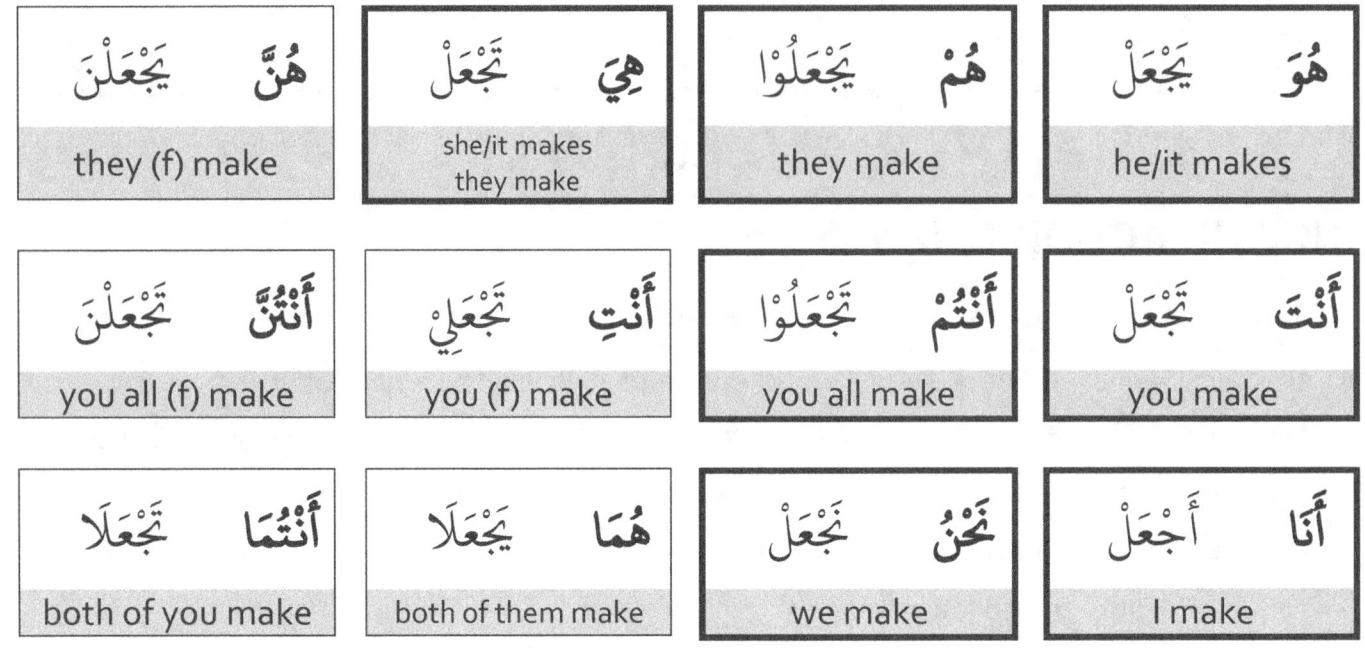

Let us make some observations about the chart above. While it may look like there is an entire new chart to learn, there are only really two changes that occur:

1. ُ becomes ْ

هو يَجْعَلُ ← يَجْعَلْ | هي/أنتَ تَجْعَلُ ← تَجْعَلْ | أنا أَجْعَلُ ← أَجْعَلْ | نحن نَجْعَلُ ← نَجْعَلْ

2. ن is dropped

هم يَجْعَلُونَ ← يَجْعَلُوا | أنتِ تَجْعَلِينَ ← تَجْعَلِي | أنتما تَجْعَلَانِ ← تَجْعَلَا

3. The plural-feminine endings stay as is

هنّ يَجْعَلْنَ ← يَجْعَلْنَ | أنتنّ تَجْعَلْنَ ← تَجْعَلْنَ

Present tense actions that go through these changes are known as *BALD ACTIONS*. This is because the ُ and ن that are normally there on the end have been shaved off, leaving the action bald.

Notice that the هم bald version ends in a اْ. This اْ is not pronounced and disappears when a pronoun is attached. For example, يَجْعَلُوا becomes يَجْعَلُوهُمْ.

HINTS FOR SPOTTING BALD ACTIONS

- <u>Look for an أ ي ت ن beginning. Remember that only the endings change in bald actions!</u>

- Look for a ْ ending   OR   ✓ Look for وا ي endings - this is what is left behind when the ن drops

 Go to Chapter 9, Drill #1: Recognizing Bald Actions.

 Go to Chapter 9, Drill #2: Distinguishing Action Forms.

Remember that two ْ in a row make an "unpronounceable" arrangement. When a bald word is followed by an الْ, the ْ will change to a ِ to facilitate flow and pronunciation.

يَجْعَلْ اللهُ ← يَجْعَلِ اللهُ

We recognize present tense actions by their beginnings and endings. However, there are **FIVE SITUATIONS** under which present tense endings change. That is what we will be studying in the upcoming chapters.

When the **ENDING IS SHAVED OFF**, the actions are what we call **BALD ACTIONS**. Bald actions will retain their beginnings (ن ت ي أ), but the endings will change.

- If the action originally ended in a ـُ, its bald version will be a ـْ
- If the action originally ended in a ن, the ن is removed leaving behind a ا/و/ي
- If the action is feminine plural (هن/أنتن), it remains as ـنْ

OUR TERM	FORMAL TERM	ARABIC TERM
bald actions	jussive	فِعْل مُضَارِع مَجْزُوم

CHAPTER 10
SCENARIO 1: SHAVING WORDS

The **first** of the five scenarios in which bald actions occur is when followed by a *SHAVING WORD*.

A *SHAVING WORD* is a word that causes the action after it to become bald. The shaving words are:

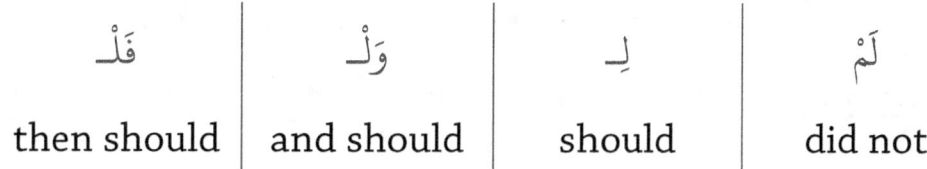

فَلْـ	وَلْـ	لِـ	لَمْ
then should	and should	should	did not

1. لم - negates the action after it and causes it to translate in the past tense

2. لِ - is used when issuing instructions; translates as "should" or "let…"

    - وَلْـ - is a combination of the connector وَ and the shaving word لِ

    - فَلْـ - is a combination of the connector فَ and the shaving word لِ

All four of the shaving words above only occur before a present tense action. They cause the action that follows it to become bald actions.

 Go to Chapter 10, Drill #1: Shaving Words.

Remember that when it comes to bald actions:

1. ُ becomes ْ

2. ن is dropped, leaving behind a ا/و/ي

3. The plural-feminine (هنّ/أنتنّ) endings stay as is

﴿٤٢﴾ ... وَيَقُولُ يَا لَيْتَنِي لَمْ أُشْرِكْ بِرَبِّي أَحَدًا 18:42

He says, "Oh, I wish I did not associate anyone with my Master!"

Notice that the word following لم is translated in the past and is negated (did not). Notice, also, the bald ending (ْ).

لِيَكْفُرُوا بِمَا آتَيْنَاهُمْ وَلِيَتَمَتَّعُوا فَسَوْفَ يَعْلَمُونَ ﴿٦٦﴾ 29:66

Let them be ungrateful for what We have given them and let them enjoy themselves, for they will soon come to know.

Though the tone is sarcastic, the ل is being used to issue instructions. Notice that the actions following the ل end in وا, indicating a missing ن.

... فَلْيَسْتَجِيبُوا لِي وَلْيُؤْمِنُوا بِي لَعَلَّهُمْ يَرْشُدُونَ ﴿١٨٦﴾ 2:186

So, they should respond to Me and they should believe in Me so that they may be guided.

The و and فل are being used to issue instructions. Notice that the actions following the shaving words end in وا, indicating a missing ن.

... وَلْيَضْرِبْنَ بِخُمُرِهِنَّ عَلَىٰ جُيُوبِهِنَّ ... ﴿٣١﴾ 24:31

And they (f) should pull their headcovers over their chests.

The ول is being used to issue instructions. Notice that there is no change to the action. This is because plural-feminine endings always stay the same.

☞ Go to Chapter 10, Drill #2: Shaving Words in Context.

OUR TERM	FORMAL TERM	ARABIC TERM
shaving words	jussive particles	حَرْف جَازِمَة لِلْمُضَارِع

CHAPTER 11
SCENARIO 2: FORBIDDING

THE FORBIDDING FORM

The **second** of the five scenarios in which BALD ACTIONS occur is the forbidding form. Forbidding is commanding someone not to do something. The forbidding form is structured as follows:

bald action + لا

أنتما لا تَجْعَلا	أنتنّ لا تَجْعَلْنَ	أنتِ لا تَجْعَلِي	أنتم لا تَجْعَلُوا	أنتَ لا تَجْعَلْ
Both of you, don't make!	You all (f), don't make!	You (f), don't make!	You all, don't make!	You, don't make!

Notice that the chart only includes five pronouns. This is because commands are most commonly issued to someone who is present. That is why all of the pronouns are in the second person (you). As we know, there are five different ways of saying the word "you" in Arabic, depending on the gender of those addressed as well as the number of people being addressed. Take note of the unique bald endings associated with each pronoun

you all (f)	you all	both of you	you (f)	you
ـْنَ	وْا	ـا	ي	ـْ

Remember that these are the endings left behind after the ة or the ن are shaved off. This applies to all forms except for the plural feminine.

👉 *Go to Chapter 11, Drill #1: Translating Forbidding Actions.*

FORBIDDING VS. NEGATION

The word لا is used not just to forbid but also to negate. Because it is used for both negating and forbidding, there is a potential to confuse them. Let us do a comparison between forbidding and negation so that we do not confuse the two.

Remember that forbidding is commanding someone not to do something.

Do not eat ramen noodles!

Negation, on the other hand, is turning an affirmative sentence into its opposite.

She eats ramen noodles. ➡ She does not eat ramen noodles.

While both structures start with a لا and are followed by a present/future tense action there is one key difference that can be used to distinguish between the two. *The action following the لا in negated sentences remain unaffected. The action following the لا in the forbidding form is always a bald action.*

Remember that when it comes to bald actions:

1. ؙ becomes ؘ

2. ن is dropped, leaving behind a ا/و/ي

3. The plural-feminine endings stay as is

لا تَأْكُلُوا	لا تَأْكُلُونَ	لا تَأْكُلْ	لا تَأْكُلُ
You all, don't eat!	You all do not eat.	You, don't eat!	You don't eat.
Forbidding	Negation	Forbidding	Negation

Notice that when the action endings remain unchanged, the structure translates as a negated sentence. When the they are bald (end in ؘ or the ن goes missing), the structure translates as the forbidding form.

 لا very rarely appears before a past tense action. When it does, however, it is always negation and never forbidding.

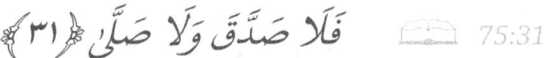

﴿٣١﴾ فَلَا صَدَّقَ وَلَا صَلَّىٰ   75:31

He did not believe, nor did he pray.

👉 Go to Chapter 11, Drill #1: Forbidding vs Negation.

FORBIDDING SOMEONE ABSENT

Note that, in English, you can only forbid someone who is present. You cannot, for example, say "He, don't do this!" In Arabic, this possibility exists, though it is not as common as forbidding someone who is present. When this happens, it translates most naturally into English as "X should not…" or "Do not let X do…"

﴿١١﴾ ... لَا يَسْخَرْ قَوْمٌ [مِّن قَوْمٍ] ...   49:11

A group of people should not mock [another group].

Do not let a group of people mock [another group of people].

Notice that the action has an outside doer. Also notice that the one being commanded (قوم) is not present.

👉 Go to Chapter 11, Drill #3: Forbidding an Absentee.

MORE ON لا

Now that you know how to distinguish between forbidding and negation, let us learn the last function of لا to ensure that there is no confusion surrounding the لا. The last function of لا is what is known as complete negation.

Complete negation is denying something emphatically and completely. It translates as "there is absolutely no…" Complete negation is easily distinguishable from the previous two forms, because, in complete negation, the لا is always followed by a noun with a ؎ label. Your chances of confusing the noun with the ﹷ label with a past tense action (e.g جَعَلَ) are very slim, since لا is very rarely followed by a past tense action. Though لا can be followed by a present tense action, present tenses actions do not end in ﹷ. This makes the complete negation structure distinct and easy to spot.

2:2 ... ﴿٢﴾ ... لَا رَيْبَ ۛ فِيهِ ...

There is absolutely no doubt in it.

لا is followed by a noun ("doubt") with a ﹷ label. Notice how it translates as "there is absolutely no...".

40:17 ﴿١٧﴾ لِيَوْمَ تُجْزَىٰ كُلُّ نَفْسٍ بِمَا كَسَبَتْ ۚ لَا ظُلْمَ الْيَوْمَ ۖ إِنَّ اللَّهَ سَرِيعُ الْحِسَابِ

Today, every soul will be compensated according to what it earned. There will be absolutely no oppression today. No doubt, Allah is swift in account.

لا is followed by a noun ("oppression") with a ﹷ label. Notice how it translates as "there is absolutely no...".

12:92 ﴿٩٢﴾ ... قَالَ لَا تَثْرِيبَ عَلَيْكُمُ الْيَوْمَ ۖ يَغْفِرُ اللَّهُ لَكُمْ

He said, "There is absolutely no blame on you today."

لا is followed by a noun ("blame") with a ﹷ label. Notice how it translates as "there is absolutely no...".

Also notice that complete negation is always followed by a TLDR phrase.

It is also possible for لا to negate nouns outside of the complete negation structure. When a noun is negated outside of the complete negation structure, it is marked by a ﹷ label and translates without the emphasis.

2:254 ﴿٢٥٤﴾ ... ۖ لَّا بَيْعٌ فِيهِ وَلَا خُلَّةٌ وَلَا شَفَاعَةٌ ...

There will be no trade, friendship, nor intercession.

☞ *Go to Chapter 11, Drill #4: لا + Noun.*

☞ *Go to Chapter 11, Drill #1: Cumulative Practice.*

When you see a لا, check if it is followed by an action or noun

If **ACTION**, check ending:

→ Normal ending = negation -> translates to "does not"

→ Bald ending = forbidding -> translates to "do not!"

If **NOUN**, check ending:

→ Marked with ﹷ = complete negation -> translates to "there is absolutely no…"

→ Marked with ﹹ = ordinary negation -> translates to "there is no…"

OUR TERM	FORMAL TERM	ARABIC TERM
forbidding	proscription/imperative	فِعْل نَهْي
negation (action)	"	فِعْل نَفْي
negation (noun)	"	لا النَّافِيَة
complete negation	categorical negation	لا النَّافِيَة لِلْجِنْسِ

CHAPTER 12
SCENARIO 3: CONDITIONAL SENTENCES

INTRODUCTION

The **third** scenario in which bald actions occur is in CONDITIONAL SENTENCES. A conditional sentence is a two part sentence. The first part of the sentence sets the condition, and the second part tells what will happen if that condition is met. The first part is known as the CONDITION, and the second part is known as the CONSEQUENCE. Conditional sentences can deal with known factors or hypothetical situations.

[If we reach a million subscribers], [we will celebrate with ice cream.]

The condition = We reach a million subscribers

The consequence = we will celebrate with ice cream

Notice that both the condition and the consequence are full sentences, and they're tied together by the conditional word ("if").

[Whenever I eat at that restaurant], [I get a stomach ache.]

The condition = I eat at the restaurant

The consequence = I get a stomach ache

Notice that both the condition and the consequence are full sentences, and they're tied together by the conditional word ("whenever").

 Go to Chapter 12 , Drill #1: Conditional Sentences - English.

THE CONDITION AND THE CONSEQUENCE

Conditional sentences in Arabic begin with one of the following words:

لَوْ	إِذَا	إِنْ
had...	when/whenever	if

BALDNESS IN CONDITIONAL SENTENCES

Although all three of these words (إنْ/إذا/لو) create conditional sentences, the only one that causes actions to become bald is إنْ. If the condition and/or consequence are present/future actions, إنْ will cause them **both** to become bald. The words إذا and لو do not cause actions to become bald.

TRANSLATING CONDITIONAL SENTENCES

As far as translation goes, <u>all actions in an إذا and إنْ sentence always translate in the present tense, even if they are past tense.</u> On the other hand, <u>all actions in a لو sentence always translate in the past tense, even if it is present.</u>

Notice how these rules apply to the example sentences below.

... فَإِن يَشَإِ اللَّـهُ / يَخْتِمْ [عَلَىٰ قَلْبِكَ] ... ﴿٢٤﴾   42:24

If Allah wills, / He could seal [your heart].

Notice that يشأ and يختم are both bald (ْـ endings).

... وَإِنْ عُدتُّمْ / عُدْنَا ... ﴿٨﴾   17:8

If you return, / We will return.

Notice that despite عدنا and عدتم being past tense actions, they are being translated in the present tense ("return", "will return").

... وَإِذَا سَمِعُوا اللَّغْوَ / أَعْرَضُوا [عَنْهُ] ... ﴿٥٥﴾   28:55

When they hear vain talk, / they keep [away from it].

Notice that despite سمعوا and أعرضوا being past tense actions, they are being translated in the present tense (hear, keep).

14:21 ... قَالُوا لَوْ هَدَانَا اللَّـهُ / لَهَدَيْنَاكُمْ ... ﴿٢١﴾

They said, "Had Allah guided us, / we would have guided you."

Notice that the past tense is translated as is because it is a لو sentence.

TIPS FOR IDENTIFYING THE CONDITION AND THE CONSEQUENCE

Remember that a conditional sentence is made up of two parts: the condition and the consequence. Identifying these two parts is relatively straightforward. The words إن/إذا/لو indicate the start of the condition. The start of the consequence can be identified by one of the following:

1. A new action, marking a new sentence
2. A ف
3. لَ on the consequence in the case of لَوْ

WHEN PAST TENSE TRANSLATES AS A PAST TENSE

Remember that the actions in a إذا and إن sentence always translate in the present tense, even if they are past tense. There is one exception to this rule: any action following the word قد in a conditional sentence translates in the past tense.

3:20 ... فَإِنْ أَسْلَمُوا فَقَدِ اهْتَدَوا ۖ وَإِن تَوَلَّوْا فَإِنَّمَا عَلَيْكَ الْبَلَاغُ ... ﴿٢٠﴾

Then if they submit, then they **have** committed to guidance. And if they turn away, then your only responsibility is delivering the message.

فَإِن كَذَّبُوكَ فَقَدْ كُذِّبَ رُسُلٌ مِّن قَبْلِكَ ... ﴿١٨٤﴾ 　3:184

But if they deny you, then other messengers **have** been denied before you.

Remember: all actions in a sentence with لو will always translate as a past tense!

... قَالُوا لَوْ نَعْلَمُ قِتَالًا / لَّاتَّبَعْنَاكُمْ ... ﴿١٦٧﴾ 　3:167

They said, "Had we known that there would be fighting,/ we would have come with you."

☞ Go to Chapter 12, Drill #2: Conditional Sentences - Arabic.

A **CONDITIONAL SENTENCE** is a two part sentence in which the first part sets the condition and the second part tells what will happen if that condition is met. The two parts are called: **THE CONDITION** and the **CONSEQUENCE**.

- Both are **FULL SENTENCES**.
- The **START OF THE CONSEQUENCE** is marked by:
    o A **NEW SENTENCE** (usually a new action)
    o A ف
        ▪ In the case of لو, it will be marked by a لَ

There are three main conditional words in Arabic.

1. إِنْ – if
    - Will **ALWAYS TRANSLATE AS PRESENT TENSE** regardless of the tense of the action following it
    - Will make a **PRESENT TENSE ACTION BALD** both in the command and the consequence

2. إِذَا – when
    - Will **ALWAYS TRANSLATE AS PRESENT TENSE** regardless of the tense of the action following it

3. لَوْ – had
    - Will **ALWAYS TRANSLATE AS PAST TENSE** regardless of the tense of the action following it
    - The **START OF THE CONSEQUENCE** is often denoted by **A** لَ

***Note that if a **CONSEQUENCE STARTS WITH** قد, it will **TRANSLATE TO THE PAST TENSE**.

OUR TERM	FORMAL TERM	ARABIC TERM
conditional sentence	conditional sentence	جُمْلَة شَرْطِيَّة
condition	protasis	شَرْط
consequence	apodosis	جَوَاب الشَّرْطِ

CHAPTER 13
SCENARIO 4: COMMANDS

INTRODUCTION

The **fourth** scenario in which bald actions occur is the commanding form. Of all the cases of bald actions, commands are the most unique. This is because they have the same endings as bald actions, but the beginnings looks different. All the cases of bald actions that we have looked at so far have had the same beginnings as present tense actions. This is not the case with commands.

اسْتَهْزِئِي	جَاهِدُوا	سَلِّمْ	**COMMAND**
لمْ تَسْتَهْزِئِي	لَمْ يُجَاهِدُوا	لم يُسَلِّمْ	**BALD**

In this chapter, we will do brief review of command endings before moving on to look at the changes that occur within the body of the commanding form.

COMMAND ENDINGS

What commands and other bald actions have in common are their endings. Although we have already studied the entire bald action chart, the only ones that we will review here are the "you" forms (second person). This is because commands can only be issued to someone who is present. Commands never appear in any other form.

you all (f)	you all	both of you	you (f)	you
ـْنَ	وْا	ـَا	ي	ـْ

Remember that the embedded pronoun is normally determined by the beginning and ending. Each of the five "you" pronouns has the same beginning and a unique ending. Since the ending is the only differentiating factor in these five pronouns, the ending is all that is needed to determine the embedded pronoun.

Though we have not yet studied the changes that occur to the beginnings in the command form, we can still determine the pronoun embedded in a command based on the ending.

 Go to Chapter 13, Drill #1: Who is Being Commanded?.

COMMAND BODY PATTERNS

Now that we are clear on command endings and embedded pronouns, let us go over the body of commands. The body is everything aside from the ending. There are three patterns that commands follow. We will study them one by one.

PATTERN 1 - THREE LETTERS OR LESS

If you see a ا followed by three letters or less, it is a command. Remember that the ending indicators do not count as original letters, nor do attached pronouns.

You, make!	You all, make!	You (f), make!	You all (f), make!	Both of you, make!
اِجْعَلْ	اِجْعَلُوا	اِجْعَلِي	اِجْعَلْنَ	اِجْعَلَا

All words in the chart above have less than three letters after the ا as well as a bald ending. These are clear signs that a word is a command. Take a look at the following examples and observe that they all start with a ا followed by three letters or less.

اِسْمَعُوا   اِرْجِعِي   اِغْفِرْ   اُدْخُلُوا   اُذْكُرُوا

اُنْظُرْ   اُحْشُرُوا   اِفْعَلُوا   اِقْتُلَا   اُذْكُرْنَ

 Go to Chapter 13, Drill #2A – Pattern #1 – Three Letters or Less.

PATTERN 2 - MORE THAN THREE LETTERS

A word that has more than three letters is a command <u>*if it has an "ii"* (ي/ــِ) *sound on the second-to-last letter of the original word.*</u>

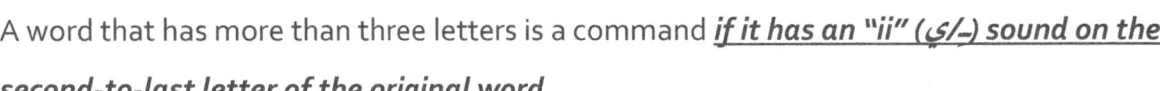

اِسْتَقِيمَا	اِسْتَقِمْنَ	اِسْتَقِيمِي	اِسْتَقِيمُوا	اِسْتَقِمْ
Both of you, be upright!	You all (f), be upright!	You (f), be upright!	You all, be upright!	You, be upright!

A ّ is an indication of two of the same letter. Keep this in mind when counting letters. The word عَلَّمَ, for example, counts as a four-letter word: ع ل ل م.

Take a look at the following examples. Observe that they all have more than 3 letters as well as an *ii* sound on the second-to-last letter of the original word.

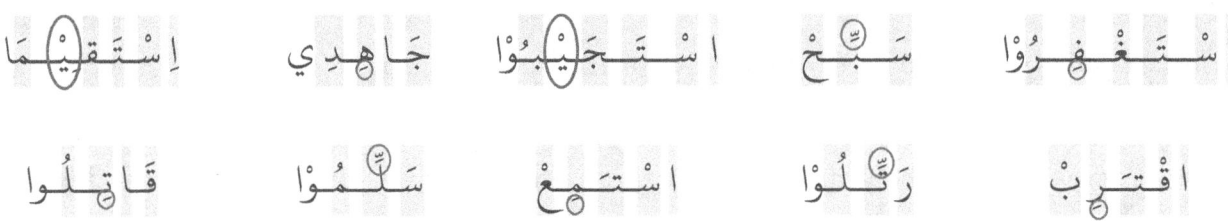

If the action has an ـَ instead of an ـِ on the second-to-last letter, it is a past tense action, NOT a command. A small difference in script makes a big difference in translation.

أنتما: سَلَّمَا	هما: سَلَّمَا	أنتنّ: سَلِّمْنَ	هنّ: سَلَّمْنَ	أنتم: سَلِّمُوا	هم: سَلَّمُوا
command	past	command	past	command	past

👉 *Go to Chapter 13, Drill #2B – Pattern #2 – More Than 3 Letters.*

PATTERN 3 - THE HYBRID

The last pattern is a hybrid between the first and second patterns. It:

1. It begins with a أ and is followed by three letters or less

2. It always has an "ii" sound (ي/ـِ) on the second-to-last letter

The first rule makes it similar to pattern one. The second rule makes it similar to pattern two. Notice, however, that this pattern always begins with an أ and not a ا. It has the addition of a ء.

أَسْلِمَا	أَسْلِمْنَ	أَسْلِمِي	أَسْلِمُوا	أَسْلِمْ
Both of you, submit!	You all (f), submit!	You (f), submit!	You all, submit!	You, submit!

Take a look at the following examples. Observe that they all beging with an أ followed by 3 letters or less. Also notice that there is an ii sound on the second-to-last letter of the original word.

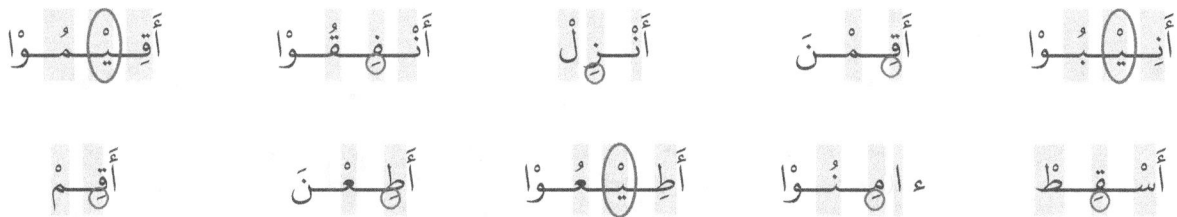

Just like pattern two actions, the past tense version of this pattern has an "aa" sound (ـَا/ا) on the second-to-last letter. When you spot a أ followed by three letters, make sure to check the mark on the second-to-last letter to determine whether it is past-tense or a command.

أنتما: أَقِيْمَا	هما: أَقَامَا	أنتن: أَقِمْنَ	هن: أَقِمْنَ	أنتم: أَقِيْمُوا	هم: أَقَامُوا
command	past	command	past	command	past

 Go to Chapter 13, Drill #2C – Pattern 3 – The Hybrid.

☞ *Go to Chapter 13, Drill #2D – Cummulative Practice.*

☞ *Go to Chapter 13, Drill #3: Command Translation Pratice.*

☞ *Go to Chapter 13, Drill #4: Cummulative Action Translation Practice.*

CONTEXT CLUES

Aside from the patterns mentioned above, there are a few additional clues that you can use to help you spot the commanding form. These clues come, not from the form of the word, but from the external context. They are particularly useful for spotting irregular actions that may not follow the three patterns listed above. Knowing these context clues serves as a shortcut that saves you the trouble of learning every irregular command pattern.

1. يا/يا أيها... - These two words are used to get someone's attention and are often followed by a command. While it is not the case the every command is preceded by يا/يا أيها, and not every يا/يا أيها is followed by a command, this makes for a quick hint that works often.

يَا أَيُّهَا الَّذِينَ آمَنُوا قُوا أَنفُسَكُمْ وَأَهْلِيكُمْ نَارًا...﴿٦﴾   66:6

O you who believe, protect yourselves and your families from a fire...

يَا أَيُّهَا الَّذِينَ آمَنُوا اتَّقُوا اللَّهَ وَذَرُوا مَا بَقِيَ مِنَ الرِّبَا إِن كُنتُم مُّؤْمِنِينَ ﴿٢٧٨﴾   2:278

O you who believe, have consciousness of God and leave usury if you are true believers.

> يَا أَهْلَ الْكِتَابِ لَا تَغْلُوا فِي دِينِكُمْ وَلَا تَقُولُوا عَلَى اللَّهِ إِلَّا الْحَقَّ ...﴿١٧١﴾ — 4:171

O people of the book, do not go overboard with regards to your faith and do not say anything but the truth about God.

2. رَبِّ/رَبَّنَا/اللَّهُمَّ - Translates as "my Lord" or "our Lord" or "oh Allah", and is used to call upon Allah. This word is often followed by the commanding or forbidding form, because the call "my Lord" is often followed by a prayer or a request.

> وَإِذْ قَالَ إِبْرَاهِيمُ رَبِّ أَرِنِي كَيْفَ تُحْيِي الْمَوْتَىٰ ...﴿٢٦٠﴾ — 2:260

When Ibrahim said, "Oh my Lord! Show me how you bring the dead to life."

> هُنَالِكَ دَعَا زَكَرِيَّا رَبَّهُ ۖ قَالَ رَبِّ هَبْ لِي مِن لَّدُنكَ ذُرِّيَّةً طَيِّبَةً ...﴿٣٨﴾ — 3:38

At that moment, Zakariyyah called upon his Lord. He said, "Oh my Lord! Gift me a righteous offspring especially from you…"

> ...رَبَّنَا تَقَبَّلْ مِنَّا ...﴿١٢٧﴾ — 2:127

"My Lord, accept from us."

3. Connectors - Connectors usually appear between two or more like things. If you spot a command followed by a connector, chances are that the next word is also a command.

> يَا أَيُّهَا الَّذِينَ آمَنُوا ارْكَعُوا وَاسْجُدُوا وَاعْبُدُوا رَبَّكُمْ وَافْعَلُوا الْخَيْرَ لَعَلَّكُمْ تُفْلِحُونَ ﴿٧٧﴾ — 22:77

O you who believe, bow down, prostrate, worship your Lord, and do good so that you may be successful.

Go to Chapter 13, Drill #5: Context Clues.

 Go to Chapter 13, Drill #6: Commands in Sentences.

ENDINGS: All commands have bald endings

you all (f)	you all	both of you	you (f)	you
ـْنَ	وا	ـا	ي	ـْ

3 COMMAND PATTERNS:

1. ا followed by three letters or less (i.e., انْظُر)
2. actions more than three letters that have a "ii" sound on the second-to-last letter* (i.e., اسْتَغْفِرْ)
3. actions that begin with أ followed by three letters with a ـِ on the second-to-last letter* (i.e., أَنْذِرْ)

   * if the action has an "aa" sound on the second-to-last letter, it is past tense

CONTEXT CLUES:

Context clues for commands are calling and connectors.

- calling (يا/يا أيها/رب/ربنا/اللهم)
- connectors

OUR TERM	FORMAL TERM	ARABIC TERM
command	interdiction/imperative	فِعْل أَمْر

CHAPTER 14
SCENARIO 5: COMMAND-CONSEQUENCE

INTRODUCTION

The **fifth and final** scenario in which bald actions occur is the command-consequence sentence. A command-consequence sentence is a two-part sentence in which a command is issued and the person being commanded is told what will happen as a consequence of them following the command.

The first part - THE COMMAND - is simply a commanding action.

The second part - THE CONSEQUENCE - is a present tense action in its bald form.

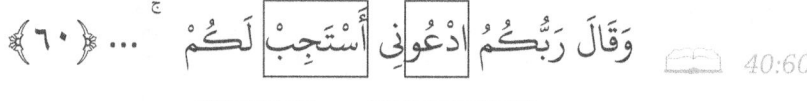

Your lord said, "Call upon me, I will respond to you."

The command: ادعو. The consequence: أستجب. Notice how the consequence is bald (ends in ـْ).

 Go to Chapter 14, Drill #1: CC in English.

IDENTIFYING THE PARTS

The COMMAND can be identified using the hints provided in the previous chapter. Remember to look for:

1. An ا followed by three letters or less

2. An "ii" sound (ي/ـِ) on the second-to-last letter on a word that is more than three letters

3. A ا followed by three letters and an "ii" sound (ي/ـِ) on the second-to-last letter

4. Context clues

The CONSEQUENCE can be identified by searching for the first bald action following the command.

TRANSLATING COMMAND-CONSEQUENCE SENTENCES

In many cases, it works simply to put a comma between the command and the consequence when translating.

2:135 وَقَالُوا كُونُوا هُودًا أَوْ نَصَارَىٰ تَهْتَدُوا ... ﴿١٣٥﴾

They said, "Be Jews or Christians, and you will be guided."

The command: كونوا (an irregular command). The consequence: تهتدوا. Notice that the consequence is bald (ن was dropped leaving behind a وا).

Sometimes, this structure translates more naturally with a "to" before the consequence. Use your judgment to arrive at the most natural translation.

15:3 ذَرْهُمْ يَأْكُلُوا وَيَتَمَتَّعُوا ... ﴿٣﴾

Leave them to eat and enjoy themselves.

RECOGNIZING A COMMAND-CONSEQUENCE

Of the five scenarios of bald actions, a command consequence is the only one that does not have a clear sign telling you why the action is bald.

1. Shaving words are a limited set of words. If you see one, you know that the action following it will be bald.

2. A forbidding action will always be preceded by a لا, making it easy to recognize

3. Conditional words are also a limited set of words, and only إن will make an action bald.

4. Commands follow specific patterns

Command-consequence does not have any such obvious sign, which makes it easy to miss. So if a word seems like it is randomly bald, chances are you missed the command-consequence. Remember that every bald action needs a reason to be bald.

 Go to Chapter 13, Drill #2: CC in Arabic.

COMMAND-CONSQEUENCE:

1. **COMMAND** – the commanding action
    - recognize using patterns from ch. 13

2. **CONSEQUENCE** – what will happen as a result if the command is followed
    - always bald
    - will transalte with a comma, an "and", or a "to"

If a word seems like it is randomly bald (no shaving word, no لا, no إنْ, doesn't follow a command pattern), then chances are it is the consequence of a command-consequence.

OUR TERM	FORMAL TERM	ARABIC TERM
command-consequence	-	أَمْر وَجَوَاب الأَمْرِ
command	interdiction	فِعْل أَمْرٍ
consequence	apodosis	جَوَاب الأَمْرِ

CHAPTER 15
Irregular Bald Actions

IRREGULAR ENDINGS

The ْ ending is a very distinctive mark of bald actions, as it rarely occurs anywhere else. Remember that the ْ on bald actions acts as a replacement for the ُ that has gone missing. There is one irregular action type, however, that never ends in a ْ. This irregular action type is the actions that end in vowels. Present tense actions that end in a vowel (ا و ي) do not have the ُ that is characteristic of ordinary present tense actions.

We have previously come across these actions in our lesson on "indicator-less actions" in Chapter 6.

يَهْدِي   يَدْعُو   يَخْشَى

Because there is no ُ that vowel-ending actions can be shaved off, these actions must be made bald in a different way. **_Actions that end in vowels are bald by removing the vowel._**

يَخْشَى ← يَخْشَ   يَدْعُو ← يَدْعُ   يَهْدِي ← يَهْدِ

☞ *Go to Chapter 15, Drill #1: Recognizing Irregular Bald Actions.*

IRREGULARS IN CONTEXT

Actions that end in vowels are quite common and they often appear in their bald form. Recall that there are five scenarios in which bald actions appear. Actions that end in vowels can - and do - appear in all five scenarios.

SCENARIO 1: SHAVING WORD

105:1 ﴿١﴾ أَلَمْ تَرَ كَيْفَ فَعَلَ رَبُّكَ بِأَصْحَابِ الْفِيلِ

Have you not seen what your Lord did to the people of the elephant?

Notice that the action is proceeded by a shaving word (لم). The original action تَرَى became تَرَ when the ى was dropped.

SCENARIO 2: FORBIDDING

28:88 ﴿٨٨﴾ ... وَلَا تَدْعُ مَعَ اللَّهِ إِلَٰهًا آخَرَ

Do not call upon any other God alongside Allah.

The original action تَدْعُو became تَدْعُ when the و was dropped.

SCENARIO 3: CONDITIONAL SENTENCES

4:133 ﴿١٣٣﴾ ... إِن يَشَأْ يُذْهِبْكُمْ أَيُّهَا النَّاسُ وَيَأْتِ بِآخَرِينَ ...

If He wills, He can do away with you all – oh people, and bring others.

The original action يَأْتِي became يَأْتِ when the ي was dropped.

SCENARIO 4: COMMANDS

43:49 ﴿٤٩﴾ ... وَقَالُوا يَا أَيُّهَ السَّاحِرُ ادْعُ لَنَا رَبَّكَ

You magician, call upon your Lord for us...

Notice that the word follows the pattern of a command (ا followed by less than 3 letters). The و was dropped, hence the ـُ ending.

SCENARIO 5: COMMAND CONSEQUENCE

12:9 ﴿٩﴾ ... اقْتُلُوا يُوسُفَ أَوِ اطْرَحُوهُ أَرْضًا يَخْلُ لَكُمْ وَجْهُ أَبِيكُمْ

Kill Joseph or abandon him somewhere, your father's attention will turn to you.

The original action يَخْلُو became يَخْلُ when the و was dropped.

 Go to Chapter 15, Drill #2: Mixed Practice.

Irregular actions are actions that end in a vowel (ا و ي).

Irregular actions show their baldness by dropping the vowel letter.

يَهْدِ ← يَهْدِي   يَدْعُ ← يَدْعُو   يَخْشَ ← يَخْشَى

OUR TERM	FORMAL TERM	ARABIC TERM
irregular action	irregular verb	فِعْل مُعْتَلّ
vowel	"	حَرْف العِلَّة

CHAPTER 16
TRIMMED ACTIONS

INTRODUCTION

Remember, bald actions are present tense actions in which the ُ ending is replaced with a ْ or the ن ending is dropped. The concept of trimmed actions is similar. In trimmed actions:

1. The ُ is replaced with a َ

2. The ن is dropped

3. The feminine plural pronouns remain the same

Notice that the ُ is replaced by an َ and not a ْ, as is the case with bald actions. The ْ is the equivalent of no mark, which is where bald actions get their name. The َ, on the other hand, is just a step below the ُ, which is why these actions are considered trimmed and not bald.

Also notice that two of the three rules are the same as they are for bald actions. Even though they look the same, you will have no trouble distinguishing between bald and trimmed actions. This is because trimmed actions only happen in one scenario.

 Go to Chapter 16, Drill #1: Translating Trimming Words.

TRIMMING WORDS

The only case in which present tense actions become trimmed is when they come after a trimming word. The trimming words are as follows:

أَنْ	لَنْ	حَتَّى	لِ/كَيْ/لِكَيْ
to/that	will not/never	until	in order/so that

28:19 ... قَالَ يَا مُوسَىٰ أَتُرِيدُ **أَن** تَقْتُلَنِي كَمَا قَتَلْتَ نَفْسًا بِالْأَمْسِ ... ﴿١٩﴾

He said, "Musa, do you intend **to** kill me like you killed someone yesterday?"

Notice that the action coming after the أن is trimmed – it ends in a َ instead of a ُ.

2:55 ... وَإِذْ قُلْتُمْ يَا مُوسَىٰ **لَن** نُّؤْمِنَ لَكَ **حَتَّىٰ** نَرَى اللَّـهَ جَهْرَةً ... ﴿٥٥﴾

Remember when you said, "Musa, we **will not** believe in you **until** we see God with our own eyes."

Notice that the action coming after لن is trimmed – it ends in a َ instead of a ُ.
The action after حتى is also trimmed, though you cannot see it – putting a َ on an ى does not make a difference in pronounciation.

28:13 ... فَرَدَدْنَاهُ إِلَىٰ أُمِّهِ **كَيْ** تَقَرَّ عَيْنُهَا وَلَا تَحْزَنَ **وَلِتَعْلَمَ** أَنَّ وَعْدَ اللَّـهِ حَقٌّ ... ﴿١٣﴾

Then We returned him to his mother **so that** she may be comforted and not grieve and **so that** she knows that the promise of Allah is true...

Notice that the word after كي is trimmed – it ends in a ﹶ instead of a ﹸ.

Notice as well that the effect of the word is carried over by و – ولا تحزن is also trimmed.

16:39 ﴿ لِيُبَيِّنَ لَهُمُ الَّذِي يَخْتَلِفُونَ فِيهِ وَلِيَعْلَمَ الَّذِينَ كَفَرُوا أَنَّهُمْ كَانُوا كَاذِبِينَ ﴿٣٩﴾

...*so that* He may clarify for them that which they differ in and *so that* those who denied may know that they were liars.

Notice that the word after لِ is trimmed – it ends in a ﹶ instead of a ﹸ.

57:23 ﴿ لِكَيْلَا تَأْسَوْا عَلَىٰ مَا فَاتَكُمْ وَلَا تَفْرَحُوا بِمَا آتَاكُمْ ۗ ﴿٢٣﴾ ...

...*so that* you do not despair over what escaped you nor be happy over what He gave you...

Notice that the word after كي is trimmed – the ن is dropped, leaving behind a وا.

Notice also that a لا can come between the trimming word and the action to negate the action ("so that you do not...").

 Go to Chapter 16, Drill #2: Trimming Words in Context.

You may also have noticed that this is not our first time seeing the word لِ. The word لِ is also a shaving word that translates as "should..." or "let..." Though the shaving word and the trimming version have different meanings, they look the same. Use the following hints to distinguish between the two:

1. If the word following the لِ has an ﹶ endings, it is the trimming version, translating as "so that...."

2. If the word following the لِ has an ﹾ endings, it is the shaving version, translating as "should...."

3. If the word following the لِ ends in وا or ي or ا, it could technically be either. Try translating it both ways to see which makes more sense in context of the ayah.

Go to Chapter 16, Drill #3: Types of لِ.

Remember the TLDR words قبل and بعد؟ Normally, a TLDR word is followed by a noun. These two words, however, are unique. They can be followed by a verb as well. This is also the case in English. You can say "before school" (TLDR + noun) as well as "before I travel" (TLDR + verb).

In Arabic, however, there is one condition that must be met if a verb is to follow the words قبل and بعد. The word أَنْ must be inserted between the two words, and acts as something of a buffer between the unlikely pair. It is also possible for ما to act as a buffer as well.

2:254 ... مِّن قَبْلِ أَن يَأْتِيَ يَوْمٌ ... ﴿٢٥٤﴾

before a day comes

3:19 ... مِن بَعْدِ مَا جَاءَهُمُ الْعِلْمُ ... ﴿١٩﴾

after knowledge came to them

Trimmed actions are a step lower than bald actions.

NORMAL	BALD	TRIMMED
ـُ	ـْ	ـَ
ـانِ/ـوْنَ/ـيْنَ	ن drops	ن drops
ـْنَ	ـْنَ	ـْنَ

Trimmed actions only happen when there is a trimming word before the action.

3 types of لِ: TLDR (to/for), trimming (so that), shaving (should)

OUR TERM	FORMAL TERM	ARABIC TERM
trimmed action	subjunctive verb	فِعْل مُضَارِع مَنْصُوْب
trimming words	subjunctive particle	حُرْف نَاصِبَة لِلْمُضَارِع

MODULE 2: MORE ON ACTIONS

BACK-TO-BACK ACTIONS

(1) كَانَ + present tense action = used to/was doing
 - كَانَ in a normal sentence = was

(2) كَادَ + present tense action = almost did
 - كَيْدُ + present tense action = almost does

(3) action + present tense action = state of being
 - will translate as -ing/while/as/-ly
 - present tense action is the state of being. Comes at the end of the sentence.

ORIGINAL ENDING	TRIMMED ENDING	BALD ENDING	IRREGULAR BALD ENDING
ـُ	ـَ	ـْ	ـُ → و ـَ → ا/ىٰ ـِ → ي
هُوَ يَضْرِبُ	نْ drop leaves behind ا/و/ي هُمَـا يَضْرِبَانِ (وْنَ) يَضْرِبُ	نْ drop leaves behind ا/و/ي يَضْرِبْ	نْ drop leaves behind ا/و/ي يَضْرِبْ
أَنْتِ تَضْرِبِينَ أَنْتُمَا (بَانِ) هُمْ (بُوْنَ)	تَضْرِبْ remains unchanged	تَضْرِبْ remains unchanged	تَضْرِبْ remains unchanged

Trimmed endings happen in **one case**: when there is a **trimming word** (أَنْ، لَنْ، كَيْ، حَتَّىٰ)

Bald endings happen in five cases:

SHAVING WORDS

فَقْ	فَقْ	لْ	فَأْ

COMMANDS

bald ending, but no أَ تَ نَ
follows three patterns:

a. ا + ≤ 3 letters
b. "ii" sound on second to last letter of an action with >3 letters
c. أَ + "ii" sound on second to last letter of an action with ≤ 3 letters

Context clues: -calling يَا أَيُّها / يَا أَيُّهم / يَا الَّذِين / يَا بَنِي
-connectors

FORBIDDING

- لا + bald ending = forbidding — Do not do that!
- لا + normal ending = negation — You do not do that.
- لا + ـَ (noun) = complete negation — There is absolutely no...
- لا + ـُ (noun) = negation — There is no...

CONDITIONAL SENTENCES

Two-part sentence: a condition and its consequence.
A consequence is marked by the start of a new sentence or a فَ

إنْ – if
makes present tense actions bald
will always translate in the present tense *

إذا – when
will always translate in the present tense*

لَوْ – had
will always translate in the past tense
consequence will often start with لَ

*if the consequence starts with فَقَدْ, then it will translate in the past tense

COMMAND-CONSEQUENCE

Do X, and Y will happen.
X = command
Y = consequence, will be bald present tense

distinguished from state of being because the action will be bald, state of being is normal

MODULE
- 3 -

ADD-ONS

An exploration of little words and phrases that commonly appear in sentences but are not a core part of the base sentence structure.

CHAPTER 17
EMPHASIS

INTRODUCTION

There are a handful of tools in Arabic that can be used to emphasize a sentence. These tools all have roughly the same meaning and serve to make a sentence sound more forceful. Though these different tools serve the same function and have the same meaning, each tool is used in a different grammatical situations. There are:

1. tools of emphasis that appear on **ALL TYPES OF WORDS**

2. tools of emphasis used **EXCLUSIVELY ON NOUNS**

3. tools of emphasis used **EXCLUSIVELY ON ACTIONS**

THE SHARED TOOL OF EMPHASIS

The first tool of emphasis we will be learning is the most flexible and the most common. It appears very often in the Quran and can appear on any type of word - nouns, adjectives, actions, and even TLDRs. This tool of emphasis is the letter ل. It always attaches to the beginning of the word and always has a ﹷ on top.

29:69 ... وَإِنَّ اللَّـهَ لَمَعَ الْمُحْسِنِينَ ﴿٦٩﴾

Certainly, Allah is [definitely] with those who excel.

Notice that the ل is on a TLDR word.

43:15 ... إِنَّ الْإِنسَانَ لَكَفُورٌ مُّبِينٌ ﴿١٥﴾

Certainly, humans are [definitely] clearly ungrateful.

Notice that the ل is on the AFTER IS.

37:151-152   ... لَيَقُولُونَ ﴿١٥١﴾ وَلَدَ اللَّـهُ وَإِنَّهُمْ لَكَاذِبُونَ ﴿١٥٢﴾

They [definitely] say, "Allah has begotten." Certainly, they are [definitely] liars.

Notice that the ل is on an action, as well as on the AFTER IS.

You may have noticed that sentences containing the ل of emphasis often contain the word إِنَّ as well, which is also an emphasizer. While it is natural to have multiple emphasizers in a single sentence in Arabic, it sounds awkward in English. For this reason, you will find that many translators ignore the ل of emphasis when translating.

Remember that the TLDR لِ becomes لَ when a pronoun attaches to it (لَهُ لَكَ لَنَا). Make sure not to confuse the TLDR لَ with the emphasis لَ. This should be easy, because the ل of emphasis never gets an attached pronoun, it only attaches to independent pronouns

---

 Go to Chapter 17, Drill #1: ل of Emphasis .

THE NOUN EXCLUSIVE TOOL OF EMPHASIS

There is one tool of emphasis that attaches only to nouns and appears only in *IS SENTENCES*. The بِ of emphasis:

1. Only appears in *IS SENTENCES* that begin with ما or ليس (negated *IS SENTENCES*)

2. Only appears on the AFTER IS

2:8   ... وَمَا هُم | بِمُؤْمِنِينَ ﴿٨﴾

They are not at all believers

Notice how the ب is not being translated as a TLDR word. Notice as well that is on the AFTER IS *(or in this case, the* IS NOT*).*

$$\text{... لَيْسَ بِخَارِجٍ مِّنْهَا ۚ ...} \langle ١٢٢ \rangle \quad 6:122$$

He <u>is</u> certainly not emerging from it.

Notice how the ب is not being translated as a TLDR word. Notice as well that is on the AFTER IS *(or in this case, the* IS NOT*).*

The most natural way to translate emphasis in a negated sentence is "…not at all…" or "…certainly not…"

NOTE ON ليس

ليس is a unique word. It is acts like a past tense action because it can conjugate (it will get the past tense indicators) and can also have an outside "doer" with a doer label. However, it translates as "is not", making it sound like an IS SENTENCE.

When approaching the translation of sentences with ليس, approach it like an ACTION SENTENCE: translate the doer first, then the action, then the receiver, then the TLDR. However, remember that the action in this case translates as "is/are not". This will make your translation sound like an IS SENTENCE.

$$\text{وَقَالَتِ النَّصَارَىٰ لَيْسَتِ الْيَهُودُ [عَلَىٰ شَيْءٍ]...} \langle ١١٣ \rangle \quad 2:113$$

And the Christians said, "<u>The Jews</u> are not [upon anything]."

Notice how ليس has an outside doer with a doer label (اليهود). Also notice that the doer translates first.

$$\text{لَيْسُوا سَوَاءً...} \langle ١١٣ \rangle \quad 3:113$$

<u>They</u> are not the same.

Notice how ليس is conjugated in the هم form, as it has the past tense ending indicator "وا". Also notice that the doer translates first.

The بِ of emphasis will never attach itself to a pronoun since a pronoun never acts as the AFTER IS.

Do not to confuse the بِ of emphasis with the TLDR بِ. Remember that the بِ of emphasis appears only in negated sentences and will only attach to the AFTER IS. If the sentence does not begin with a ما or ليس, there will be no بِ of emphasis.

 Go to Chapter 17, Drill #2: بِ of Emphasis.

THE ACTION EXCLUSIVE TOOL OF EMPHASIS

The last tool of emphasis that we will learn is one that is exclusive to present/future tense actions. The نَّ of emphasis:

1. Attaches to the **end** of present/future tense actions

2. Is most often used together with the لَ of emphasis

3. Always translate as "will definitely" (future tense)

14:13   ... لَنُخْرِجَنَّكُم مِّنْ أَرْضِنَا ... ﴿١٣﴾

We will most definitely expel you from your land.

Notice that the ن is at the end of the action, it is accompanied by أ, and that the action is translated in the future tense ("we will...").

Notice that, unlike the أ and بِ, the نّ attaches to the end. This is very significant, because the نّ affects the standard ending of the action when it attaches. Recall the beginnings and *endings* of present/future actions tell us what embedded pronoun is contained within. **<u>To be able to correctly identify the embedded pronoun in an emphasized action, it is necessary to understand how the addition of the نّ affects the endings.</u>**

Here is what you need to know:

1. The نّ knocks off the وْنَ ending and replaces it with a ـُ

2. The نّ knocks off the ـُ ending and replaces it with a ـَ

تُخْرِجُوْنَ	يُخْرِجُوْنَ	أُخْرِجُ	نُخْرِجُ	تُخْرِجُ	يُخْرِجُ
↓	↓	↓	↓	↓	↓
تُخْرِجُنَّ	يُخْرِجُنَّ	أُخْرِجَنَّ	نُخْرِجَنَّ	تُخْرِجَنَّ	يُخْرِجَنَّ

Notice that whenever the original ending is an ـُ, it gets replaced with an ـَ. Whenever the original ending is an وْنَ, it gets replaced with a ـُ. The beginnings stay the same. Use the beginning and the modified versions of the original endings to determine the embedded pronoun.

PRONOUN	ENDING	BEGINNING
هُوَ	ـَنَّ	ـيـ
هُمْ	ـُنَّ	

		ت
هِيَ أَنْتَ	۔نَّ	
أَنْتُمْ	۔نُّ	

		أ
أَنَا	۔نَّ	

		نـ
نَحْنُ	۔نَّ	

نّ ON FORBIDDING ACTIONS

When a لا comes before a نّ verb, it is a stern form of forbidding. Emphasized forbidding words in the Quran most commonly occur in the أَنْتَ and أَنْتُمْ forms. The forms are the same, the only difference being that the action is preceeded by a لا.

لا تُخْرِجُنَّ

don't you (pl.) dare expel

لا تُخْرِجَنَّ

don't you dare expel

3:102 ... وَلَا تَمُوتُنَّ إِلَّا وَأَنْتُم مُّسْلِمُونَ ﴿١٠٢﴾ ...

Don't you (dare) die except as believers.

☞ Go to Chapter 17, Drill #3: نّ of Emphasis.

لَ

- Appears on all types of words: nouns, actions, TLDRs
- Do not confuse with TLDR word. Never has an attached pronoun, only an independent pronoun.

بِ

- Appears only in sentences negated with ما or ليس
- Appears only on the AFTER IS
- Do not confuse with the word. Never has an attached pronoun.
- Translates as "not at all"

***ليس is unique. It is an action that translates as "is not". When translating, translate doer -> action.

نَّ

- Appears at the end of present/future actions
- Used in conjunction with لَ
- Translates as "definitely will" (future tense)
- ـنَّ means the ending used to be an وْنَ
- ـنَّ means the ending used to be a ـُ
- If proceeded by لا, it will be a forbidding action, translates as "don't you dare…"

OUR TERM	FORMAL TERM	ARABIC TERM
emphasis	stylistic intensification	تَوْكِيْد
لَ of emphasis	-	لام التَّوْكِيْدِ
بِ of emphasis	-	بَاء الزَّائِدَة
نَّ of emphasis	-	نُوْن التَّوْكِيْد

CHAPTER 18
THE واو

INTRODUCTION

We were introduced briefly to the connector واو in a previous chapter. The word واو has a handful of meanings. In this chapter, we will revisit the connector واو and be introduced to three additional meanings for the word واو. The four types of واو are:

1. Connector واو
2. Oath واو
3. Starter واو
4. While واو

CONNECTOR واو

The connector واو, as you know, translates as "and" and is the most common connector word in Arabic. The connector واو can join two (or more) words, two (or more) fragments, or two (or more) sentences.

1. **Words** - When connecting words, the connector واو acts as a transmitter, carrying over the same ending label. As long as two or more words are joined by a واو, they are considered part of the same grammatical unit.

   38:45   وَاذْكُرْ عِبَادَنَا إِبْرَاهِيمَ وَإِسْحَاقَ وَيَعْقُوبَ ... ﴿٤٥﴾

   Remember our servants Abraham, Isaac, and Jacob

   Notice the transmission of the ؘ labels. All are part of the same grammatical unit, acting as receivers.

2. **Fragments** - As long as two or more fragments are joined by a واو, they are considered part of the same grammatical unit. If the fragments start with a word that accepts a

label, the واو acts as a transmitter, carrying the label over to the first word in the next fragment.

9:24 ﴿ قُلْ إِن كَانَ آبَاؤُكُمْ وَأَبْنَاؤُكُمْ وَإِخْوَانُكُمْ وَأَزْوَاجُكُمْ وَعَشِيرَتُكُمْ ... ﴿٢٤﴾

Say, "If your parents, your children, your siblings, your spouses, and your extended family..."

The واو is connecting a series of possessive fragments, all of which are acting as a doer for كَانَ. The first word in a possessive fragment takes a ـُ label. Notice the ـُ label transmitting.

23:22 ﴿ وَعَلَيْهَا وَعَلَى الْفُلْكِ تُحْمَلُونَ ﴿٢٢﴾

You all are carried upon them (cattle) and upon ships.

Most TLDR words do not accept labels, so there is no transmition.

3. **Sentences** - The connector واو can connect two ACTION SENTENCES, two IS SENTENCES, or an ACTION SENTENCE and an IS SENTENCE.

28:25 ﴿ ... فَلَمَّا جَاءَهُ وَقَصَّ عَلَيْهِ الْقَصَصَ ... ﴿٢٥﴾

When he came to him and told him his story...

ACTION SENTENCE + ACTION SENTENCE

43:85 ﴿ ... لَهُ مُلْكُ السَّمَاوَاتِ وَالْأَرْضِ وَمَا بَيْنَهُمَا وَعِندَهُ عِلْمُ السَّاعَةِ وَإِلَيْهِ تُرْجَعُونَ ﴿٨٥﴾

To Him belongs whatever is in the skies and the earth and whatever is between them, and to Him belongs the knowledge of the hour, and you will be returned to Him.

IS SENTENCE + IS SENTENCE + ACTION SENTENCE

OATH واو

The واو can also sometimes translate as "I swear by..." or "by..." It is used to swear by something. The oath واو can be distinguished from the connector واو by looking at the word following the واو. The word following an oath واو always has a ِ label on it.

وَالْعَصْرِ ﴿١﴾ إِنَّ الْإِنسَانَ لَفِي خُسْرٍ ﴿٢﴾   103:1-2

I swear by time, certainly man is in loss.

Notice the ِ label on the word after the و. Also, notice how the و – a single letter – is translated.

... قَالُوا وَاللَّـهِ رَبِّنَا مَا كُنَّا مُشْرِكِينَ ﴿٢٣﴾   6:23

They said, "We swear by Allah, our Lord, that we were not polytheists."

Notice the ِ label on the word after the و. Also, notice how the و – a single letter – is translated.

The oath واو most commonly appears in Juz 30 at the beginning of a handful of surahs. Outside of Juz 30, the phrase والله occurs a handful of times.

☞ *Go to Chapter 18, Drill #1: Oaths.*

STARTER واو

The واو can sometimes be used to start a new sentence or a new idea. The concept of a starter واو is similar to the concept of capitalizing the first letter of a sentence in English. It is not translated, and is simply there to indicate the start of a new idea.

مَثَلُ الْفَرِيقَيْنِ كَالْأَعْمَىٰ وَالْأَصَمِّ وَالْبَصِيرِ وَالسَّمِيعِ ۚ هَلْ يَسْتَوِيَانِ مَثَلًا ۚ أَفَلَا تَذَكَّرُونَ ﴿٢٤﴾ وَلَقَدْ أَرْسَلْنَا نُوحًا إِلَىٰ قَوْمِهِ إِنِّي لَكُمْ نَذِيرٌ مُّبِينٌ ﴿٢٥﴾   11:24-25

These two groups are like the blind and the deaf as compared to the hearing and the seeing. Are they equal? Do you not think? _We sent Noah to his people saying, "I am certainly a clear warner for you."

The topic of the two ayaat are unrelated. The و indicates the start of a new sentence and a new idea. It is not translated.

This واو is fairly frequent in the Quran. A واو is most likely acting as a starter if:

1. A واو appears at the beginning of an ayah

2. Sounds odd if translated with "and"

The oath واو, like the starter واو, appears at the beginning of an ayah for the most part. The word following it, however, will always have a ؘ label. Meanwhile, the starter واو is never followed by a word with the ؘ label.

WHILE واو

Remember that a state of being, also known as an adverb, is used to inform the listener about the state of someone/something as an action occurs. The واو can sometimes act as a state of being. When it does, it will be followed by a full sentence that starts with a pronoun. Together, the واو and the sentence that follows it act as the state of being.

Just like the state of being that we studied in chapter 8, this واو can translate as "while", "as", "in a state of", or "-ly". It will also appear at the end of the sentence, just as the state of being does.

... الَّذِينَ يَمُوتُونَ [وَهُمْ كُفَّارٌ] ... ﴿١٨﴾

4:18

...those who die [while disbelievers]...

...those who die [as disbelievers]...

...those who die [in a state of disbelief]...

3:75 ﴿٧٥﴾ ... وَيَقُولُونَ عَلَى اللَّـهِ الْكَذِبَ [وَهُمْ يَعْلَمُونَ] ...

They speak lies about Allah [while knowing].

They speak lies about Allah [knowingly].

This type of واو is most likely to be confused with the connector واو because the while واو may look like it is connecting two sentences. To distinguish between the two, simply ask yourself if there are two things happening concurrently. If the answer is yes, it is a while واو. In the first example above, the people are dying WHILE disbelieving. The two actions are happening at the same time. In the second example above, the people are lying WHILE knowing that they are doing so. The two actions are happening at the same time.

The following is an example of a connector واو that may be mistaken for a while واو.

3:85 ﴿٨٥﴾ وَمَن يَبْتَغِ غَيْرَ الْإِسْلَامِ دِينًا فَلَن يُقْبَلَ مِنْهُ وَهُوَ فِي الْآخِرَةِ مِنَ الْخَاسِرِينَ

Whoever seeks a religion other than Islam, then it will not be accepted from him and he will be from amongst the losers in the next life.

It is not the case that "it will not be accepted from them WHILE they are losers in the afterlife". Each of the two sentences is an independent statement. The two things are not happening at the same time.

 *Go to Chapter 18, Drill #2: While.*

Go to Chapter 18, Drill #3: Type of واو.

Connector

- Can connect words, fragments, or sentences
- When connecting words and fragments, all connected portions act as a single grammatical unit
- Transmits labels when connecting words and when connecting fragments (except for TLDR phrases, which do not have labels)
- Can connect two like sentences or two differing sentences

Oath

- The word after the واو always takes a ِ label
- Translates as "I swear by..." or "by..."
- Most often appear at the beginning of surahs in Juz 30
- Sometimes والله or وَرَبِّكَ appear in other surahs

Starter

- Begins new sentences and ideas, is not translated

While

- Translates as "while," "in a state of," "as," or "-ly"
- Occurs as the last part of a sentence
- Is most often followed by a sentence that starts with a pronoun

OUR TERM	FORMAL TERM	ARABIC TERM
connector	conjunction	وَاو العَطْفِ
oath	-	وَاو القَسْمِ
starter	-	وَاو الاسْتِئْنَافِ
while	adverb	وَاو الحَالِيَّة

CHAPTER 19
TEMPLATES

INTRODUCTION

Oftentimes, studying the grammatical breakdown of a sentence or fragment can help a language learner understand the meaning of that structure. There are other cases, however, in which there is a disconnect between the theory and the application. It is in such cases that templates become useful. A template is a preset form for certain types of sentences. Rather than going through the pains of studying the technicalities that will not necessarily lead you to understanding, it is simpler to learn the structure as a set template. We will be studying four such templates in this chapter.

IT IS NOT APPROPRIATE...

The following template is used to express the idea that it would not be appropriate or befitting for someone to behave a certain way or commit a certain action.

مَا كَانَ لِـ(PERSON) أَنْ [ACTION]

It would not be appropriate for (PERSON) to [ACTION].

 3:161   ﴾١٦١﴿ ... وَمَا كَانَ (لِنَبِيٍّ) أَن [يَغُلَّ]

It would not be befitting for a (Prophet) to [cheat].

24:16   ﴾١٦﴿ ... مَّا يَكُونُ لَـ(نَا) أَن [نَّتَكَلَّمَ] بِهَٰذَا ...

It is not appropriate for (us) to [talk] about this.

☞ Go to Chapter 19, Drill #1: It is Not Appropriate.

148

X WOULD NOT BE ONE TO...

The following template is used to express the idea that someone is not the type to commit a certain action.

مَا كَانَ (PERSON) لِـ[ACTION]

(PERSON) would not be one to [ACTION].

29:40 … وَمَا كَانَ (اللَّهُ) لِـ[يَظْلِمَ]ـهُمْ ﴿٤٠﴾

(Allah) would not be one to [oppress] them.

7:43 … وَمَا كُـ(نَّا) لِـ[نَهْتَدِيَ] لَوْلَا أَنْ هَدَانَا اللَّهُ ﴿٤٣﴾

(We) would not have been the type to [commit to guidance] had Allah not guided us.

Notice that in this example, the (person) portion of the template is an embedded pronoun. This is also possible.

 Go to Chapter 19, Drill #2: X Would Not Be One to Y.

You may have noticed that this template is very similar to the previous. However, there is one key difference. Notice that in the previous template, the لِ is followed directly by a *noun*. In this template, the لِ is followed directly by a *trimmed action*. To distinguish between the two templates, pay attention to what is attaching to the لِ.

 Go to Chapter 19, Drill #3: Differentiating Between the Templates.

NOTHING BUT.../ONLY...

This template is a bit different than the previous two in that it does not involve a completely new structure. Rather, it involves add-ons that are inserted into the an ordinary sentence. This add-on is the "nothing but..." add-on, and can appear both in IS SENTENCES and ACTION SENTENCES.

You are a messenger -> You are **_nothing but_** a messenger

They tell lies -> They tell **_nothing but_** lies

The Arabic versions of this add-on are إن+إلا and ما+إلا (they are synonymous). The template pattern is as follows:

- The إن/ما always appears at the beginning of the sentence
- In IS SENTENCES, the إلا appears between the BEFORE IS and AFTER IS
- In ACTION SENTENCES, the إلا appears between the action and the doer/receiver

23:35 ﴿٢٣﴾ إِنْ أَنتَ إِلَّا نَذِيرٌ

You are nothing but a warner.

18:5 ﴿٥﴾ ...إِن يَقُولُونَ إِلَّا كَذِبًا

They say nothing but lies.

11:40 ﴿٤٠﴾ وَمَا آمَنَ مَعَهُ إِلَّا قَلِيلٌ

None believed alongside him but a few.

This add-on can also translate as "only..." The alternative to the above translations would be:

You are only a warner.

They only tell lies.

Only a few believed alongside him.

You may use whichever translation you feel is more natural.

 Go to Chapter 19, Drill #4: Only/Nothing But.

X IS ENOUGH AS...

This template is used to express the idea that someone/something suffices for a certain role.

كَفَىٰ بِـ(PERSON) [ROLE]ًا

(PERSON) is enough/suffices as a [ROLE].

4:45 ... وَكَفَىٰ بِـ(اللَّـهِ) [نَصِيرًا] ﴿٤٥﴾

(Allah) is enough as [an ally].

Notice that the role has the ً label. Notice also that the بِ does not translate!

46:8 ... وَكَفَىٰ بِـ(ـهِ) [شَهِيدًا] بَيْنِي وَبَيْنَكُمْ ﴿٤٥﴾

(He) is enough as [a witness] between me and you

Notice that the role has the ً label. Notice also that the بِ does not translate!

 Go to Chapter 19, Drill #5: X is Enough as Y.

IT IS NOT APPROPRIATE

مَا كَانَ لِـ (PERSON) أَنْ (ACTION)

X WOULD NOT BE ONE TO

مَا كَانَ (PERSON) لِـ (ACTION)

HINT: لِـ + noun = not appropriate

لِـ + action = would not be one to

NOTHING BUT/ONLY (إن + إلا، ما + إلا)

Added to normal *IS SENTENCES* and *ACTION SENTENCES*

- إن/ما comes at beginning of the sentence
- إلا comes after the *ACTION* or the *AFTER IS*

PERSON IS SUFFICIENT AS A ... (كفى بـ)

- Person is attached to the بِـ
- The role will have the ـً label

MODULE 3: ADD-ONS

There is no conceptual thread that runs through this module. Each chapter stands alone.

EMPHASIS
Words that are added on in order to highlight something.

لَ
- can come on nouns, actions, or TLD words
- TLD لَ gets a ـِ (except for pronouns), emphasis gets a ـَ
- translates as "definitely"

ن
- comes on AFTER IS in sentences negated by ما or ليس*

  *acts like an action that translates as "is not" – it has an outside or embedded "doer"
- translates as "not at all"

ن
- comes on present tense actions
- will usually come with لَ of emphasis
- will translate as future tense ("will definitely")
- *if it is proceeded by لا, it is usually an emphatic forbidding (don't you dare)
- changes تَفْعَلُ -> تَـ and ـُ -> ـَ

THE و CONNECTOR
- Connects words, fragments, and sentences
- when connecting words and fragments, it acts as a single grammatical unit
- transmits labels
- can connect two like sentences or two differing sentences

OATH
- the following word takes ـِ labels
- will translate as "I/we swear by", depending on the context

STARTER
- begins new sentences and ideas, like capitalizing a letter
- does not translate

WHILE
- translates as "while", "in a state of", "as" or "-ly"
- occurs as the last part of a sentence
- usually followed by a sentence that starts with a pronoun

TEMPLATES

(1) It is not appropriate for (PERSON) to (ACTION)   ما كانَ لِ(PERSON) أنْ (ACTION)

(2) (PERSON) would not be one to (ACTION)   ما كانَ (PERSON) لِ(ACTION)

HINT: لِ + noun = not appropriate
لِ + action = would not be one to

(3) Nothing but/only
can come on both is sentences and action sentences

(4) (PERSON) is enough as a (X)   كَفى بِ(PERSON) (X)ـاً

MODULE
- 4 -

WORD PATTERNS

A brief deviation away from the world of sentences and into the world of words - the study of Arabic word forms and patterns that multiplies one's vocabulary base

CHAPTER 20
The Agent

INTRODUCTION

The subject of most of our studies so far has been how words come together to form larger grammatical structures. We have not studied much in the way of the words themselves. In the world of linguistics, Arabic is most famous for its templatic system for words. Many words in Arabic follow specific templates, each producing a unique meaning. The benefits of learning these patterns are twofold. They can:

1. Help you expand your vocabulary by equipping you with the tools to extrapolate the meanings of words you have not specifically memorized

2. Help you recognize certain grammatical structures that only include words that follow specific patterns.

In this chapter, we will be learning some of the most frequently used word patterns as well as the grammar structures in which they are most commonly used.

THE AGENT

The word "to write" is an action and a "writer" is someone who writes.

The word "to sing" is an action and a "singer" is someone who sings.

The word "to teach" is an action and a "teacher" is someone who teaches.

Notice how the addition of the "-er" suffix can transform an action into the agent that carries that action out. This is the idea behind word pattern formation. Many words can be derived from a common base through the addition of prefixes, suffixes, or even indicators within the body of the word.

The agent is one of the most commonly used word patterns in Arabic. There are two patterns that the agent follows.

PATTERN 1: MU-II

The agent is marked by the prefix مُ as well as an "ii" sound (ي/ِ) on the second to last letter of the word.

مُبِـــيْـــنٌ	مُسْلِمٌ	مُنافِقٌ	مُكَذِّبٌ
one who clarifies	one who submits	hypocrite	denier

Notice that all of these words start with a مُ and have an "ii" sound (ي/ِ) on the second to last letter. These two elements stay consistent regardless of the other changes that occur in the word. That is because these are the two elements that represent this pattern. Also notice that all of these words translate as an agent - someone who does something.

The "ii" sound (ي/ِ) appears on the second to last letter of the **original** word. The ون،ين،ات labels that commonly attach to nouns do not count as part of the original word. When looking for the "ii" sound (ي/ِ) on the second to last letter, make sure to first ignore the ending labels.

TRACING IT BACK TO THE ACTION

If you are having a difficult time figuring out what action an agent is related to, you can follow this process to help you trace it back.

1. Remove all extras from the agent   المُنْذِرِيْنَ ← مُنْذِر
2. Replace the مُ with a يُ   مُنْذِر ← يُنْذِر
3. The result is the present tense version of the action   يُنْذِر

☞ *Go to Chapter 20, Drill #1: Mu-ii Agent Pattern.*

PATTERN 2: AA-I

The agents can also be marked by a ا as the second letter and a ِ on the third letter.

ظَالِمٌ	صَادِقٌ	كَاذِبٌ	كَافِرٌ
oppressor	honest person	liar	disbeliever

Notice that all of these words have a ا as the second letter and a ِ on the third letter. These two elements stay consistent regardless of the other changes that occur in the word. That is because these are the two elements that represent this pattern. Also notice that all of these words translate as an agent - someone who does something.

☞ *Go to Chapter 20, Drill #2: Aa-ii Agent Pattern.*

TRACING IT BACK TO THE ACTION

If you are having a difficult time figuring out what action an agent is related to, you can follow this process to help you trace it back.

1. Remove all extras from the agent   الخَالِقُوْنَ ← خَالِق
2. Remove the ا   خَالِق ← خ ل ق
3. The resulting three letters are the letters of the past tense   خَلَقَ

THE AGENT VS THE DOER

<u>Do not confuse the agent with the doer. The agent is like any noun and can play the role any noun can play.</u> Though it sounds like both the agent and the doer describe someone who carries out an action, remember that the agent refers to a word pattern while the doer

refers to the role a word plays in a larger sentence. Again, the agent is just a word pattern and can, as a matter of fact, play any number of roles in a sentence.

For example, the word "writer" follows the agent word pattern, but the usage of the word in a sentence is versatile. The sentences below show the agent (writer) appearing as a RECEIVER, a BEFORE IS, and a DOER.

I met a writer [at the job fair] [yesterday].
The word "writer" is playing the role of RECEIVER.

That writer is very skilled.
The word "writer" is playing the role of the BEFORE IS.

A famous writer wrote the script [for that movie].
The word "writer" is playing the role of the DOER.

This is the case in Arabic as well. The two agent patterns that we studied can only tell us how to translate the word itself. It can, however, fit into a sentence in a number of ways.

25:8 ... وَقَالَ الظَّالِمُونَ إِن تَتَّبِعُونَ إِلَّا رَجُلًا مَّسْحُورًا ﴿٨﴾

The oppressors said, "You are only following a bewitched man."

ظالم follows agent pattern #2. The agent is playing the role of the DOER.

3:57 ... وَاللَّـهُ لَا يُحِبُّ الظَّالِمِينَ ﴿٥٧﴾

Allah does not love the oppressors.

ظالم follows agent pattern #2. The agent is playing the role of the RECEIVER.

2:254

﴿وَالْكَافِرُونَ هُمُ الظَّالِمُونَ ٢٥٤﴾ ...

The disbelievers are the oppressors.

ظالم follows agent pattern #2, as does كافر. There are two agents in this sentence: one is playing the role of the BEFORE IS, the other is playing the role of the AFTER IS.

☞ *Go to Chapter 20, Drill #3: Cummulative Practices.*

THE AGENT AS AN ADVERB

An adverb is a word that describes the circumstance or manner in which an action was conducted. In other words, it describes the state of someone/something as an action happens.

I tiptoed *quietly* into the room.

The word "quietly" described the circumstance or manner in which the action "tiptoed" was conducted. This makes it an adverb.

We have come across the adverb – also known as the state of being – twice before:

1. When there are two back-to-back actions in one sentence (Ch. 8)

2. The while واو (Ch. 18)

Agents can also act as adverbs in Arabic. This is the last type of adverb that we will be studying.

It goes without saying that not every agent is acting as an adverb. Here is how you can spot an agent that is acting as an adverb:

1. It will always have a receiver label (ةً ءً ينَ اتٍ اتٍ)

2. It will never have an ال

3. It comes at the end of a sentence (minus TLDRs, as their position is flexible)

4. It translates as "as", "while", "-ly", "-ing"

48:27 ۞ ...لَتَدْخُلُنَّ الْمَسْجِدَ الْحَرَامَ إِنْ شَاءَ اللَّهُ آمِنِينَ... ﴿٢٧﴾

You will definitely enter the sacred mosque -- if God wills -- <u>safely</u>.

- It follows the aa-i agent pattern (آمِن = عَامِن)
- It has the receiver label (ين)
- It does not have an ال
- It is at the end of the sentence

وَذَا النُّونِ إِذ ذَّهَبَ مُغَاضِبًا... ﴿٨٧﴾

Remember Jonah, when he left <u>angrily</u>...

- It follows the agent pattern (مُ + ‒)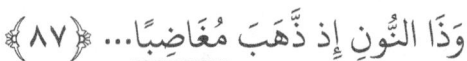
- It has a receiver label (ً)
- It doesn't have an ال
- It is at the end of the sentence

 Go to Chapter 20, Drill #4: Agent Adverb.

 Though agents are the most common forms in which adverbs appear, adverbs can sometimes be ordinary words as well. However, they will still appear with the same labels as ordinary adverbs and describe a circumstance or manner, just as ordinary adverbs do.

4:79 ۞ ...وَأَرْسَلْنَاكَ لِلنَّاسِ رَسُولًا... ﴿٧٩﴾

We sent you to the people <u>as a messenger</u>.

THE AGENT – a word pattern to express one who does something

- Pattern 1 - starts with مُ and an "ii" sound (ي/ـِ) on the second to last letter

- Pattern 2 - has a ا as the second letter and a ـِ on the third letter

- Not to be confused with the doer - can play any role in a sentence

- Often used adverbially

    - has receiver label (ـًا/ـَا، ـَيْن، ـِيْنَ، اتِ/اتٍ)

    - does not have ال

    - will be at the end of the sentence

    - Translates as "as", "while", "-ly", "-ing"

OUR TERM	FORMAL TERM	ARABIC TERM
agent	active participle	اِسْم فَاعِل
adverb	"	حَال (اِسْم مُفْرَد)

CHAPTER 21
THE TARGET

THE TARGET

The target is the opposite of the agent. While the agent is the pattern used to represent someone/something that **carries out** an action, the target pattern is used to represent someone/something that is **affected by** an action. For example, the word "punisher" is an agent, and the word "punished" is a target. It represent someone or something affected by the action of punishment.

The target is a commonly used pattern in Arabic. There are two patterns that the target follows.

PATTERN 1: MU-AA

The target is marked by the prefix مُ as well as an "aa" sound (١/َ) on the second to last letter of the word. ***Make sure not to confuse this with the agent, which is marked by an "ii" sound (ـِ/ي) on the second to last letter!***

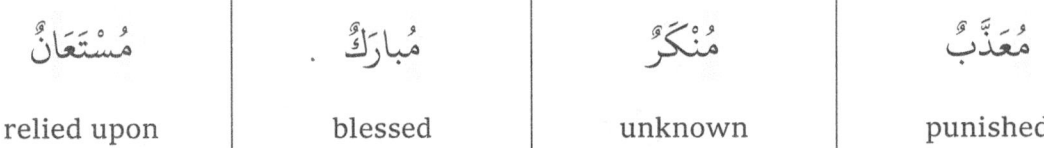

مُسْتَعَانٌ	مُبارَكٌ	مُنْكَرٌ	مُعَذَّبٌ
relied upon	blessed	unknown	punished

Notice that all of these words begin with a مُ and have an "aa" sound (١/َ) on the second to last letter. These two elements stay consistent regardless of the other changes that occur in the word. That is because these are the two elements that represent this pattern. Also notice that all of these words translate as a target - someone/something on the receiving end of an action.

TRACING IT BACK TO THE ACTION

If you are having a difficult time figuring out what action a target is related to, you can follow this process to help you trace it back.

4. Remove all extras from the target   المُسْتَعَانُ ← مُسْتَعَان

5. Replace the مُ with a يُ   مُسْتَعَان ← يُسْتَعَان

6. The result is the present passive version of the action   يُسْتَعَان

 Go to Chapter 21, Drill #1: Mu + aa Target Pattern.

PATTERN 2: MA-U

The target can also be marked by the prefix مَ as well as a و as the second-to-last letter.

مَأْكُوْلٌ	مَكْتُوْبٌ	مَظْلُومٌ	مَعْلُومٌ
eaten	written	oppressed	known

Notice that all of these words begin with a مَ and have a و as the second-to-last. These two elements stay consistent regardless of the other changes that occur in the word. That is because these are the two elements that represent this pattern. Also notice that all of these words translate as a target- someone/something on the receiving end of an action.

TRACING IT BACK TO THE ACTION

If you are having a difficult time figuring out what action a target is related to, you can follow this process to help you trace it back.

4. Remove all extras from the target   مَخْلُوْقَاتٍ ← مَخْلُوْق

5. Remove the مَ and the و   مَخْلُوْق ← خ ل ق

6. The resulting three letters are the letters of the past tense   خَلَقَ

 Go to Chapter 21, Drill #2: Ma-u Target Pattern.

THE TARGET VS THE RECEIVER

<u>Do not confuse the target with the receiver. A target is like any other noun and can play any role that a noun can play.</u> Though it sounds like both describe someone/something on the receiving end of an action, remember that the target refers to a word pattern while the receiver refers to the role a word plays in a larger sentence. Again, the target is just a word pattern and can, as a matter of fact, play any number of roles in a sentence.

For example, the word "oppressed" is a target, but the usage of the word in a sentence is versatile. The sentences below show the target (oppressed) appearing as a DOER, a BEFORE IS, and a RECEIVER.

The oppressed <u>rebelled</u> [against the rulers].
The word "the oppressed" is playing the role of the DOER.

The oppressed <u>are</u> very upset.
The word "the oppressed" is playing the role of the BEFORE IS.

The rulers <u>mocked</u> the oppressed.
The word "the oppressed" is playing the role of the RECEIVER.

This is the case in Arabic as well. The two target patterns that we studied can only tell us how to translate that specific word. It can fit into a sentence in a number of ways.

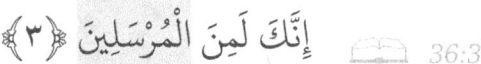

إِنَّكَ لَمِنَ الْمُرْسَلِينَ ﴿٣﴾   36:3

Certainly, you are from those who have been sent.

مُرْسَل follows target pattern #1. The target here is the noun after a TLDR phrase.

15:61 فَلَمَّا جَاءَ آلَ لُوطٍ الْمُرْسَلُونَ ﴿١٥﴾

When those who were sent came to the people of Lot.

مُرْسَل follows target pattern #1. The target here is playing the role of the doer.

👉 *Go to Chapter 21, Drill #3: Cummulative Practice.*

THE TARGET AS AN ADVERB

Recall that an adverb is a word that describes the circumstance or manner in which an action was conducted. We learned in the previous chapter that in Arabic, adverbs often follow the agent pattern. Adverbs sometimes also follow the target pattern.

 17:13 ... وَنُخْرِجُ لَهُ يَوْمَ الْقِيَامَةِ كِتَابًا يَلْقَاهُ مَنشُورًا ﴿١٣﴾

On the day of judgement, we will bring forth a book for him that he will find <u>spread open</u>.

"Spread open" describes the circumstance of the book/ the manner in which the person will find the book. Also notice that:

1. *It is marked by one of the receiver labels*
2. *Does not have a ال*
3. *Comes at the end of a sentence*

These are the same rules that apply when the agent acts as an adverb.

👉 *Go to Chapter 21, Drill #4: Target Adverbs.*

 Though agents and targets are the most common forms in which adverbs appear, adverbs can sometimes be ordinary words as well. However, they will still appear with the same labels as ordinary adverbs and describe a circumstance or manner, just as ordinary adverbs do.

📖 4:79 ...وَأَرْسَلْنَاكَ لِلنَّاسِ رَسُولًا... ﴿٧٩﴾

We sent you to the people as a messenger.

THE TARGET – word pattern that expresses one who is affected by an action

- Pattern 1: starts with a مُ and has an "aa" sound (ا/َ) on the second to last letter

- Pattern 2: starts with a مَ and has a و as the second-to-last letter

- Not to be confused with the receiver - can play any role in a sentence

- Often used adverbially

    1. has receiver label (ةً/ـًا، ـيْنِ، ـيْنَ، ـاتِ/ـاتٍ)
    2. does not have ال
    3. will be at the end of the sentence
    4. translates as "-ly", "-ed", "as", or "while"

OUR TERM	FORMAL TERM	ARABIC TERM
target	passive participle	اِسْم مَفْعُوْل
adverb	"	حَال (اِسْم مُفْرَد)

CHAPTER 22
COMPARATIVES

THE COMPARATIVE

A comparative, as the name suggests, is a word used to compare two things or two groups of things. Some examples of comparatives in English are: better, faster, sharper, stronger, bigger, and taller. Notice that comparatives in English are usually marked by an -er suffix. Comparatives in Arabic also follow a set pattern.

أَحْسَنُ	أَكْثَرُ	أَظْلَمُ	أَكْبَرُ
better	more	more oppressive	bigger

Notice that all of these words begin with a ‎أ followed by three letters. These elements do not change because they are the elements that represent this pattern.

There are only two comparatives that do not follow this pattern, and they are the words خَيْر and شَرّ, which translate as "better" and "worse". Note that these words can also translate as "good" and "bad". These are the only words that double up as comparatives and ordinary words.

 Go to Chapter 22, Drill #1: Comparative Patterns.

Comparatives can be used in a number of different ways, all of which produce different meanings.

BETTER THAN...

You will find that sentences containing comparatives are often structured as follows:

item 1	is	comparative	+	than	+	item 2
Honey	is	better		than		sugar

Comparatives in Arabic follow an almost identical structure. When the word مِنْ appears with a comparative, it translates as "than".

item 1 [is] comparative + مِنْ + item 2

… وَإِثْمُهُمَا أَكْبَرُ مِنْ نَفْعِهِمَا … ﴿٢١٩﴾   2:219

Their harm is greater than their benefit.

Item 1: their harm   comparative: great*er*   than: مِنْ   item 2: their benefit

As you read the Quran, you will likely notice that sentences including comparatives often exclude item 2. This is done deliberately so as to leave the statement general. When a sentence does not specify item 2, the implication is that item 1 is better than are too many to ennumerate.

اللّٰهُ أَكْبَرُ

Allah is greater.

… وَرِزْقُ رَبِّكَ خَيْرٌ وَأَبْقَىٰ ﴿١٣١﴾   20:131

*The provision of your Lord is <u>**better and more lasting**</u>.*

… وَلَأَجْرُ الْآخِرَةِ أَكْبَرُ ۚ لَوْ كَانُوا يَعْلَمُونَ ﴿٤١﴾   16:41

*The reward of the hereafter is <u>**greater**</u>. If only they knew…*

☞ *Go to Chapter 22, Drill #2: X is Better Than Y.*

BETTER IN TERMS OF...

In Arabic, sentences that compare one thing to another will often include a qualifying statement explaining in what way item 1 is more than item 2. The addition made to the sentence below explains in what way honey is better than sugar.

Honey is better than sugar <u>as far as healthy eating goes</u>.

In Arabic, the qualifier:

1. appears after the comparative
2. is a noun with the ً label
3. is always general
4. will usually translate as "in terms of" or "in"

... أَنَا أَكْثَرُ مِنكَ [مَالًا] وَأَعَزُّ [نَفَرًا] ﴿٣٤﴾   18:34

I am <u>greater</u> than you [in terms of wealth] and <u>more honorable</u> [in lineage].

... هُوَ أَشَدُّ مِنْهُ [قُوَّةً] وَأَكْثَرُ [جَمْعًا] ﴿٧٨﴾   28:78

He is <u>greater</u> than him [in strength] and <u>greater</u> [in terms of resources].

☞ *Go to Chapter 22, Drill #3: In Terms of....*

WHO IS MORE..

Comparatives in the Quran are also frequently used as part of a rhetorical question. This template begins with the question word مَنْ and is followed by a comparative.

... وَمَنْ أَصْدَقُ مِنَ اللَّـهِ قِيلًا ﴿١٢٢﴾   4:122

Who is <u>more truthful</u> in their speech than God?

Notice that the مَنْ is followed by a comparative. Notice also that this sentence contains a qualifier (قِيلًا is a general noun coming after a comparative with the ـَ label).

The مِنْ in this template is often followed by a مَنْ in which case it will be written as مِمَّنْ and translate as "than the one who". It is always followed by a full sentence.

11:18 ﴿١٨﴾ ... وَمَنْ أَظْلَمُ مِمَّنِ افْتَرَىٰ عَلَى اللَّـهِ كَذِبًا

Who is **more wrongdoing** than the one who fabricates lies against God?

Notice how مِمَّنْ is followed by a full ACTION SENTENCE. Notice also how it translates.

 Go to Chapter 22, Drill #4: Who is More... .

BEST...

While comparatives are used to compare the quality of two items, superlatives express that an item is of the highest degree of quality. Some examples of superlatives are: best, fastest, tallest, biggest, and most. There are two cases in which the comparative form translates as a superlative.

CASE 1 - ال

The first case in which a comparative translates as a superlative is when ال is added to the beginning.

87:1 ﴿١﴾ سَبِّحِ اسْمَ رَبِّكَ **الْأَعْلَى**

*Declare the perfection of your Lord - the **most high**.*

92:15 ﴿١٥﴾ لَا يَصْلَاهَا إِلَّا **الْأَشْقَى**

*Only the **most wicked** will enter it.*

CASE 2 - POSSESSIVE

The second case in which a comparative translates as a superlative is when it appears as the item in a possessive fragment.

7:17 ﴿١٧﴾ ... وَلَا تَجِدُ **أَكْثَرَهُمْ** شَاكِرِينَ

You will find **most of them** ungrateful.

39:18 الَّذِينَ يَسْتَمِعُونَ الْقَوْلَ فَيَتَّبِعُونَ **أَحْسَنَهُ** ... ﴿١٨﴾

...those who listen to what is said and follow the **best of it**...

Note that this structure does not always translate with an "of" in between the two words, even though it is technically a possessive fragment. There are cases in which the translation must be made to sound natural in the target language, as in the example below.

40:57 ... وَلَـٰكِنَّ **أَكْثَرَ النَّاسِ** لَا يَعْلَمُونَ ﴿٥٧﴾

...however, **most people** do not know...

☞ *Go to Chapter 22, Drill #5: Comparative or Superlative.*

☞ *Go to Chapter 22, Drill #6: Cummulative Practice.*

THE COMPARATIVE

- Pattern: starts with أَ, followed by three letters

- When a comparative is followed by مِنْ, it translates as "than" rather than "from"

- Can be followed by a qualifier explaining how item 1 is better than item 2. The qualifier will always be a general noun with the ً label. Translates as "in terms of" or "in".

- Can be used in a rhetorical question: who is more x than… (وَمَنْ…مِنْ…).

    o وَمَنْ…مِمَّنْ occurs often and means "who is more x than the one who…"

- Translated as a superlative when:

    o accompanied by an ال

    o in a possessive fragment

OUR TERM	FORMAL TERM	ARABIC TERM
comparative	"	اِسْم تَفْضِيْل
qualifier	accusative of specification	تَمْيِيْز

CHAPTER 23
IDEAS

THE IDEA

Ideas express the abstract, intangible noun related to an action. Words like education, justice, and creation are intangible and are associated with certain actions. They are different than words like brick, kite, or pen, for example, which are tangible and are not derived from a verb.

teaches → education
acts justly → justice
creates → creation

There are more than twenty word patterns in Arabic used for the idea, as compared to the 1-2 patterns associated with the agent, the target, and the comparative. For this reason, it is actually easier to identify ideas based on their definitions rather than their patterns.

The idea, like the other word types we have studied, can play any number of roles in a sentence, but also appears in some specific grammatical constructions.

 Go to Chapter 23, Drill #1: Idea-ntification.

THE WHY

Take a look at the following sentences.

I discipline my children [out of love for them].

We avoid processed sugar [for health reasons].

That boy does not study [out of laziness].

The bracketed parts all serve one common purpose in the sentences. They tell you why the action took place. This is what we call THE WHY, because it is used to explain why an action occurred.

The conditions for THE WHY in Arabic are as follows:

1. it must be an idea

2. it will have the ً label

3. it will never have an ال

4. it will always come at the end of a sentence (excluding TLDRs)

THE WHY will usually translate as "in order to...", "because", or "out of".

9:92 ﴿... وَأَعْيُنُهُمْ تَفِيضُ مِنَ الدَّمْعِ حَزَنًا أَلَّا يَجِدُوا مَا يُنفِقُونَ ﴿٩٢﴾

Their eyes overflow with tears <u>out of sadness</u> that they cannot find anything to contribute.

The word حَزَنًا means "sadness," and is an idea. It has the receiver label ً and explains why their eyes are overflowing with tears. Notice how it translates ("out of sadness").

2:272 ﴿... وَمَا تُنفِقُونَ إِلَّا ابْتِغَاءَ وَجْهِ اللَّـهِ ... ﴿٢٧٢﴾

You only spend <u>in order to seek</u> the pleasure of Allah.

The word ابْتِغَاءَ means "pursuit," and is an idea. It has the receiver label ً and explains why they spend money. Notice how it translates ("in order to seek").

Remember, the best way to recognize an idea is to know the meaning of the word.

☞ *Go to Chapter 23, Drill #2: The Why.*

THE EMPHASIZER

Take a look at the following sentences.

Her children [completely] destroyed the house.

We [totally] forgot about the appointment.

I studied [hard] for that test.

The bracketed parts of the sentences all serve one common purpose. They are used to emphasize the action. Omitting them would not change the core meaning of the sentence – it would only make the sentence less intense. This is what we call THE EMPHASIZER, as it is used to emphasize the sentence.

The conditions for THE WHY in Arabic are:

1. it must be an idea **_that matches the action in root letters_**

2. it will have the ً label

3. it will never have ال

4. it will always come at the end of a sentence (excluding TLDRs)

Notice that the rules for THE WHY and THE EMPHASIZER are all the same except for one key difference: THE EMPHASIZER matches the action in root letters. The matching makes THE EMPHASIZER easy to spot.

56:4-5 إِذَا رُجَّتِ الْأَرْضُ رَجًّا ﴿٤﴾ وَبُسَّتِ الْجِبَالُ بَسًّا ﴿٥﴾

When the earth is shaken **severely** and the mountains are crushed **completely**.

Notice that the emphasizer is at the end of the sentence, is an idea, is general, has the ً label, and matches the action (رُجَّتْ رَجّ)

175

73:8   وَاذْكُرِ اسْمَ رَبِّكَ وَتَبَتَّلْ إِلَيْهِ **تَبْتِيلًا** ﴿٨﴾

*Mention the name of your lord and devote yourself to him **wholeheartedly**.*

Notice that the emphasizer is at the end of the sentence, is an idea, is general, has the ـً label, and matches the action (تَبَتَّلْ تَبْتِيلًا)

4:164   ... وَكَلَّمَ اللَّـهُ مُوسَىٰ **تَكْلِيمًا** ﴿١٦٤﴾

*Allah **actually** spoke to Musa*

Notice that the emphasizer is at the end of the sentence, is an idea, is general, has the ـً label, and matches the action (كَلَّمَ تَكْلِيمًا)

Notice that in each of the examples above, the emphasis is translated differently. There is no single formula for how to capture the emphasis in translation. The way the emphasis is translated depends on the action. You would not, for example, say that someone spoke completely or that they shook wholeheartedly. Use your sense and judgement when translating, and do not hesitate to refer to a translation if you get stuck.

 Go to Chapter 23, Drill #3: The Emphsizer.

The Idea

- Intangible idea associated with a verb

- Recognized in Arabic based on meaning, not pattern

- **The why:** tells us why an action takes place. It will always be an idea, be general, have the ؎ label, and come at the end of the sentence. It will usually translate as "out of", "because", or "in order to".

- **The emphasizer:** emphasizes an action. It will always be an idea that matches the action in root letters, be general, have the ؎ label, and come at the end of the sentence. Translates is flexible depending on the context.

OUR TERM	FORMAL TERM	ARABIC TERM
idea	infinitive	مَصْدَر
the why	causative object	مَفْعُوْل لَهُ/مَفْعُوْل لِأَجْلِهِ
the emphasizer	cognate accusative	مَفْعُوْل مُطْلَق

MODULE 4: WORD PATTERNS

Many words in Arabic follow specific patterns, each producing a unique meaning.

	TARGET	**AGENT**	**COMPARATIVE**	**IDEA**
	one who carries out an action	one who is affected by an action	compares two things	expresses intangible idea associated with an action
DOES THIS WORD...				
...ACT AS AN ADVERB?	✓	✓	✗	✗
...FOLLOW A SPECIFIC PATTERN?	✓	✓	✓	✗
	pattern #1: ﹹ + ii sound pattern #2: aa + ii	pattern #1: ﹹ + aa sound pattern #2: ﹹ + و	أ + 3 letters	no pattern, recognized by meaning

an adverb will always:
(1) be at the end of the sentence
(2) have a receiver label
(3) will not have ال
(4) will translate as "-ly", "while", "as", "-ing"

Though the idea does not follow a specific pattern, recognizing it is important because it can play two unique roles in a sentence:

Explains **why** an action is taking place:
- will be an idea
- will have the ـِ label
- will be general
- will come at the end of a sentence (minus TLDRs)
- translates as "out of", "because of", or "in order to"

Emphasizes or **describes** and action
- will be an idea that matches the action
- will have the ـَ label
- will be general
- will come at the end of a sentence (minus TLDRs)
- translation is flexible

MODULE
- 5 -

COMPLEX STRUCTURES

An examination of full sentences or fragments that act like nouns - nouns that are longer and more elaborate than ordinary nouns

CHAPTER 24
Complex Nouns

INTRODUCTION

In this chapter, we will explore the idea of the COMPLEX NOUN. COMPLEX NOUNS are nouns that are longer and more elaborate than normal nouns. Though these nouns look different than the ordinary nouns that we are accustomed to, they function more or less like ordinary nouns.

I met **the founder of the company.**

I met **the one who founded a million dollar company with just $200 of startup capital.**

Compare the two sentences above. The receiver in both sentences is highlighted. Notice however, that the receiver in the first sentence is a simple fragment. The receiver in the second sentence is much longer and more elaborate. They both answer the question, "who did you meet?", and are therefore both the receivers. Yet the second receiver is much more elaborate. It is a COMPLEX NOUN.

We use and hear COMPLEX NOUNS in English all the time. Now we will be learning how to spot and translate them in Arabic. In order to be able to do this, we will study:

1. The inner mechanics and workings of COMPLEX NOUNS

2. COMPLEX NOUNS as a part of different types of fragments and sentences

 Go to Chapter 24, Drill #1: Identifying Complex Nouns - English.

THE MECHANICS OF THE COMPLEX NOUN

Complex nouns in Arabic are made up of two parts.

1. They always begin with one of the following five words:

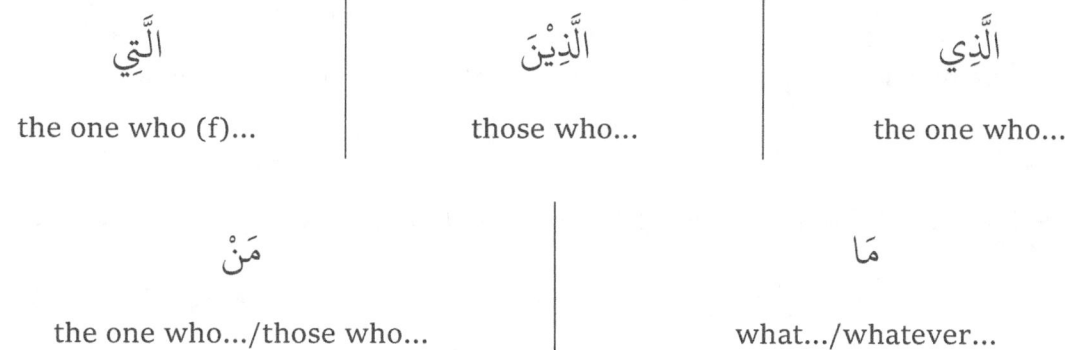

الَّتِي	الَّذِينَ	الَّذِي
the one who (f)...	those who...	the one who...

مَنْ	مَا
the one who.../those who...	what.../whatever...

2. They are then followed directly by either:

   a) A full sentence (can be either an ACTION SENTENCE or an IS SENTENCE)

   b) A TLDR phrase

These two elements combined make a COMPLEX NOUN. Let us look at some examples.

📖 21:91 وَالَّتِي [أَحْصَنَتْ فَرْجَهَا]

the one who [guarded her chastity]

Notice that the sentence following the complex noun is a full ACTION SENTENCE.

📖 70:27 وَالَّذِينَ [هُم مِّنْ عَذَابِ رَبِّهِم مُّشْفِقُونَ]

those who [are fearful of the punishment of their Lord]

Notice that the sentence following the complex noun is a full IS SENTENCE.

📖 2:116 مَا [فِي السَّمَاوَاتِ وَالْأَرْضِ]

whatever [is in the skies and the earth]

Notice that the sentence is followed by a TLDR phrase.

Remember that these two elements come together to form a COMPLEX NOUN. They cannot be separated. Use the following hints to help you correctly determine the boundaries of a COMPLEX NOUN.

1. The following words mark the **beginning** of a COMPLEX NOUN: الذي، الذين، التي، ما، من

2. Remember that the second part of a COMPLEX NOUN is either made up of an ACTION SENTENCE, an IS SENTENCE, or a TLDR phrase. To find where the COMPLEX NOUN **ends**, simply look for the end of the sentence or the TLDR phrase. The first word or fragment that is not related to what comes before it marks the **end** of the COMPLEX NOUN.

A NOTE ON TRANSLATION: THE AWKWARD PRONOUN

You may have noticed that the second part of a COMPLEX NOUN sometimes includes a pronoun that sounds awkward to translate. It is standard in Arabic for this pronoun to be included. You may even have heard Arabs who are non-native English speakers using this pronoun when speaking English. However, since it does not sound natural in English, simply exclude it from your translation.

... صِرَاطَ الَّذِينَ أَنْعَمْتَ عَلَيْ[ـهِمْ] ﴿٧﴾   1:7

the path of those whom you blessed [them].

... وَهُوَ الَّذِى إِلَيْ[ـهِ] تُحْشَرُونَ ﴿٧٢﴾   6:72

He is the one who you will be returned to [him].

 Go to Chapter 24, Drill #2: Mechanics.

COMPLEX NOUNS IN CONTEXT

Now that we are familiar with the inner workings of a COMPLEX NOUN and we know how to determine its boundaries, let us study COMPLEX NOUNS in context. As mentioned previously,

COMPLEX NOUNS function more or less like ordinary nouns. We will do a brief review of the functions of ordinary nouns as we study the functions of COMPLEX NOUNS.

COMPLEX NOUNS IN FRAGMENTS

We studied five fragments, all of which contain nouns. Of these five fragments, COMPLEX NOUNS can appear in four. They can appear in TLDR phrases, sentence starter fragments, possessive fragments, and descriptive fragments. They do not appear in pointer fragments.

① TLDR PHRASES

Recall that a TLDR phrase is made up of a TLDR word followed by a noun. This structure is no different when it comes to COMPLEX NOUNS.

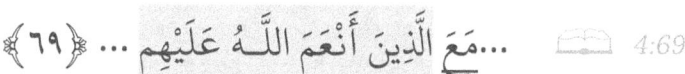

...مَعَ الَّذِينَ أَنْعَمَ اللَّـهُ عَلَيْهِم ... ﴿٦٩﴾

<u>with</u> those who Allah blessed

When the TLDR word عن precedes the complex nouns ما and مَن, it is contracted to عَمَّا and عَمَّن, respectively.
When مِن precedes them, it is contracted to مِمَّا and مِمَّن, respectively.

② SENTENCE STARTER FRAGMENTS

Sentence starter fragments are made up of a sentence starter followed by a noun. This structure is no different when it comes to COMPLEX NOUNS.

إِنَّ الَّذِينَ لَا يَرْجُونَ لِقَاءَنَا ... ﴿٧﴾   10:7

<u>Certainly</u>, those who do not wish to meet Us...

Remember that a TLDR phrase can come straight after a sentence starter, in which case the *is* will go after the TLDR phrase.

... إِنَّ لِلَّـهِ | مَا فِي السَّمَاوَاتِ وَالْأَرْضِ ... ﴿٦٤﴾ 10:55

Certainly, Allah has whatever is in the skies and the earth.

*(Lit., Certainly, for Allah **is** whatever is in the skies and the earth.)*

③ POSSESSIVE

Unlike TLDR phrases and sentence starter fragments, possessive fragments are made up of two unique nouns. The first noun is general and the second is specific. COMPLEX NOUNS are always specific, which is why they only ever appear as the second noun - the owner.

... صِرَاطَ الَّذِينَ أَنْعَمْتَ عَلَيْهِمْ ... ﴿٧﴾ 1:7

the path [of] those whom you blessed

Notice that there is a general noun before the complex noun.

... قَوْلَ الَّذِينَ كَفَرُوا ... ﴿٣٠﴾ 9:30

the words [of] those who disbelieved

Notice that there is a general noun before the complex noun.

If you see a general noun before a COMPLEX NOUN, you have yourself a possessive fragment.

The fragment translates like any other possessive fragment, so when translating, simply insert an "of" between the first noun and the COMPLEX NOUN.

④ DESCRIPTIVE

Remember that the two words in a descriptive fragment match in generality or specificity. COMPLEX NOUNS are always specific. **This means that they can only be used to describe specific nouns.**

⟨٧٧⟩ ... الْقَوْمِ الَّذِينَ كَذَّبُوا بِآيَاتِنَا ... 　21:77

the nation that denied Our signs

Notice that the word before the complex noun is specific.

⟨٢٣⟩ ... سُنَّةَ اللَّهِ الَّتِي قَدْ خَلَتْ مِن قَبْلُ ... 　48:23

the law of God that has occurred before

Notice that the fragment before the complex noun is specific. Remember that words can be specific even when they do not have an ال. In this case, the "law" is not a random law but the law of Allah. This makes it specific and not general.

If you see a specific noun followed by a COMPLEX NOUN, you have yourself a descriptive fragment. REMEMBER: a descriptor can describe a possessive fragment.

When translating, be sure to insert a "who" or "which" in between the specific noun and the COMPLEX NOUN to ensure that it translate as a descriptive fragment.

The complex nouns ما and مَنْ never act as descriptions, as it does not make sense.

When determining what role a complex noun is playing, always check to see if it is part of a fragment before checking to see if it is playing a role on the sentence level. Starting small and moving up helps streamline the process.

Go to Chapter 24, Drill #3: Complex Nouns in Fragments.

COMPLEX NOUNS IN SENTENCES

Complex nouns can appear both in ACTION SENTENCES and IS SENTENCES. They can act as the doer, receiver, BEFORE IS, or AFTER IS. **The first step in narrowing down these option is determining whether the sentence is an "action sentence" or an "is sentence".** Once you have done that, use the following strategies to narrow the options down even further.

BEFORE IS/AFTER IS

If it is the first thing that appears in a sentence, it is the BEFORE IS. If it is not the first thing that appears in an IS SENTENCE, it is the AFTER IS.

16:96 ۞ ...وَمَا عِندَ اللَّـهِ | بَاقٍ...﴿٩٦﴾

What Allah has *is* lasting.

2:284 ۞ لِلَّـهِ | مَا فِي السَّمَاوَاتِ وَمَا فِي الْأَرْضِ ... ﴿٢٨٤﴾

To Allah belongs whatever is in the skies and the earth.
(lit. For Allah *is* whatever is in the skies and the earth.)

DOER/RECEIVER

Labels are the means by which we usually identify the doer and receiver. COMPLEX NOUNS, however, do not accept labels. This means that we will have to identify them through other means. We will use a combination of clues and common sense to accomplish this. These clues should sound familiar as they are the same clues we used when we studied words that do not accept labels (like موسى and عيسى).

HINT ①

It is not often that both the doer and receiver are COMPLEX NOUNS. If you are able to identify one, you have identified the other.

11:67 … ﴿٦٧﴾ وَأَخَذَ الَّذِينَ ظَلَمُوا الصَّيْحَةُ

The loud blast took those who oppressed.

Since the doer's spot is already taken by الصيحة (it has the doer label ُ), the complex noun can only be a receiver.

2:89 … فَلَمَّا جَاءَهُم مَّا عَرَفُوا / كَفَرُوا [بِهِ] … ﴿٨٩﴾

When that which they recognized came to them, / they denied it.

The role of the receiver is filled by the attached pronoun (هم), so the complex noun can only be playing the role of doer.

HINT ②

If the doer is embedded, there cannot be an outside doer. This means that the COMPLEX NOUN word must be the receiver.

7:64 … وَأَغْرَقْنَا الَّذِينَ كَذَّبُوا بِآيَاتِنَا … ﴿٦٤﴾

We drowned those who denied our signs

Since the doer is embedded (أغرقنا = نحن), the complex noun can only be the receiver.

2:14 … وَإِذَا لَقُوا الَّذِينَ آمَنُوا / قَالُوا آمَنَّا … ﴿١٤﴾

When they meet those who believe, they say, "We believe."

Since the doer is embedded (لقوا = هم), the complex noun can only be the receiver.

HINT ③

Commands cannot have outside doers. Any COMPLEX NOUN following a command is a receiver.

﴿ ٢٥ ﴾ ... وَبَشِّرِ الَّذِينَ آمَنُوا وَعَمِلُوا الصَّالِحَاتِ أَنَّ لَهُمْ جَنَّاتٍ تَجْرِي مِن تَحْتِهَا الْأَنْهَارُ 2:25

Give good news to those who believe and do good that they will have gardens under which rivers flow.

﴿ ٢٢ ﴾ احْشُرُوا الَّذِينَ ظَلَمُوا وَأَزْوَاجَهُمْ وَمَا كَانُوا يَعْبُدُونَ 37:22

Gather those who oppressed and their likes and that which they used to worship.

HINT ④

If the action is passive, it is a substitute doer.

﴿ ٢٣ ﴾ ... وَأُدْخِلَ الَّذِينَ آمَنُوا وَعَمِلُوا الصَّالِحَاتِ جَنَّاتٍ تَجْرِي مِن تَحْتِهَا الْأَنْهَارُ 14:23

Those who believe and do good will be admitted into gardens under which rivers flow.

﴿ ٧٨ ﴾ ... لُعِنَ الَّذِينَ كَفَرُوا مِن بَنِي إِسْرَائِيلَ [عَلَىٰ لِسَانِ دَاوُودَ وَعِيسَى ابْنِ مَرْيَمَ] 5:78

Those who denied from amongst the Israelites were cursed [on the tongue of David and Jesus, the son of Mary].

HINT ⑤

A complex noun following the word قال is always the doer.

﴿ ١١٨ ﴾ ... وَقَالَ الَّذِينَ لَا يَعْلَمُونَ "لَوْلَا يُكَلِّمُنَا اللَّهُ" 2:118

Those who do not know said, "Why does Allah not speak to us?"

5:118 ... فَقَالَ الَّذِينَ كَفَرُوا مِنْهُمْ "إِنْ هَٰذَا إِلَّا سِحْرٌ مُّبِينٌ" ﴿١١٠﴾

..._then those who disbelieve_ said, "This is nothing but clear magic."

HINT ⑥

Pay attention to the meaning and use common sense

3:19 وَمَا اخْتَلَفَ الَّذِينَ أُوتُوا الْكِتَابَ إِلَّا [مِن بَعْدِ مَا جَاءَهُمُ الْعِلْمُ] ... ﴿١٩﴾

Those who were given the book did not dispute until [after knowledge came to them].

The first step in determining the role a complex noun is playing is figuring out what type of sentence it is in. Be careful not to confuse what is INSIDE the complex noun with what is AROUND it.

هُوَ | الَّذِي خَلَقَكُمْ

He **is** the one who created you.

Even though there is an action INSIDE the complex noun, that does not change the fact that this sentence is an _IS SENTENCE_. Once you have boxed off the complex noun, ignore what is INSIDE it and focus on what is AROUND it.

 Go to Chapter 24, Drill #4: Complex Nouns in Sentences.

 _Go to Chapter 24, Drill #5: Cummulative Practice._

1. **FIND BOUNDARIES** of complex noun and box it off
   - الذي، الذين، التي، ما، من marks **BEGINNING**
   - **END OF SENTENCE/TLDR PHRASE** marks end

2. Check to see if it is **PART OF A FRAGMENT**
   - Preceded by a TLDR word = TLDR phrase
   - Preceded by a sentence starter = sentence starter fragment
   - Preceded by a general noun = possessive fragment
   - Preceded by a specific noun = descriptive fragment

3. IF it is *not* part of a fragment, check to see if it is **PART OF A SENTENCE**
   - Is it an *IS SENTENCE*?
     → Appearing first: BEFORE IS
     → Appearing second: AFTER IS
   - Is it an *ACTION SENTENCE*?
     → If you have identified one part, you have identified the other
       - Does the action have an embedded doer? -> complex noun is **receiver**
       - Is it a command? -> complex noun is **receiver**
       - Is the action passive? -> complex noun is **substitute doer**
       - Does it come after قال? -> complex noun is **doer**

     ***Use common sense!!

4. Translate according to the role
5. Ignore "awkward" pronoun in translation (if applicable)

OUR TERM	FORMAL TERM	ARABIC TERM
complex noun	relative pronoun	اِسْم مَوْصُوْل وصِلَة المَوْصُوْلِ
awkward pronoun	anaphor	عَائِد

CHAPTER 25
COMPLEX DESCRIPTORS

INTRODUCTION

Complex descriptors, also known as complex adjectives, are descriptors that are longer and more elaborate than normal descriptors. Compare the two sentences below. In both sentences, the word "milk" has a descriptor, but in the second sentence, the descriptor is longer and more complex.

I only drink warm milk.

I only drink milk that has been heated and mixed with turmeric and honey.

We use and hear complex descriptors in English all the time. Now we will be learning how to spot and translate them in Arabic.

 Go to Chapter 25, Drill #1: Identifying Complex Descriptors – English.

THE MECHANICS OF A COMPLEX DESCRIPTOR

A complex descriptor is always either an ACTION SENTENCE or an IS SENTENCE. **Complex descriptors can only be used to describe general words.** If you see a general word followed directly by a sentence, you have yourself a complex descriptor.

Take a look at the following examples.

a nation that believes

قوم *is a general word and it is followed by a full* ACTION SENTENCE *(remember, a single action counts as a full sentence since the core parts of an* ACTION SENTENCE *are present: action and doer). Observe how the complex noun is translating (a nation **that**...)*

رَجُلٌ [افْتَرَى عَلَى اللهِ كَذِبًا]

a man who fabricated lies against God

رجل *is a general word followed by a full* ACTION SENTENCE. *Observe how the complex description is translating (a man **who**...).*

أَرْضٌ [فِيْهَا مَاءٌ]

a land in which there is water

أرض *is a general word followed by a full* IS SENTENCE. *Observe how the complex description is translating (a land in **which**...)*

Notice that this structure is made up only of a general noun and a sentence acting as a complex descriptor. There is no "who" or "that" in between the two in the original Arabic. These must be added into the translation. Even though they do not exist in the original Arabic, it is the convention to have them in English. Remember, a translation should always make sense in the target language.

 Go to Chapter 25, Drill #2: Translating Complex Descriptors.

Now let us take a look at complex descriptors in sentences.

وَمَا مُحَمَّدٌ إِلَّا رَسُولٌ [قَدْ خَلَتْ مِن قَبْلِهِ الرُّسُلُ] ... ﴿١٤٤﴾ 3:144

Muhammad is only a messenger [before whom messengers have passed].

*We have previously seen that a new action = new sentence. However, the sentence (*قد خلت...*) is preceded by a general word (*رسول*), turning the sentence into a complex description.*

*Notice that the noun + its complex descriptor ("a messenger before **whom** messengers have passed") is playing the role of the AFTER IS.*

21:10 لَقَدْ أَنزَلْنَا إِلَيْكُمْ كِتَابًا [فِيهِ ذِكْرُكُمْ] ۗ أَفَلَا تَعْقِلُونَ ﴿١٠﴾

We have certainly sent down a book [in which there is advice for you all]. So do you not understand? كتاب is a general word followed by a full IS SENTENCE ("there is advice") turning the sentence into a complex description.

Notice that the noun + its complex descriptor are playing the roll of the receiver.

THE AWKWARD PRONOUN

Just like COMPLEX NOUNS, COMPLEX DESCRIPTORS contain pronouns that should not be translated. While they are standard in Arabic, they do not sound normal in English. Always make sure that your translations sound natural in the target language.

3:144 ﴿١٤٤﴾ ... الرُّسُلُ [قَبْلِـهِ مِن خَلَتْ قَدْ] رَسُولٌ إِلَّا مُحَمَّدٌ وَمَا

Muhammad is only a messenger whom messengers have passed before ~~him~~

21:10 ﴿١٠﴾ تَعْقِلُونَ أَفَلَا ۗ ذِكْرُكُمْ [فِيـهِ] كِتَابًا إِلَيْكُمْ أَنزَلْنَا لَقَدْ

We have certainly sent down a book that there is advice in ~~it~~ for you all. So do you not understand?

SPOTTING A COMPLEX DESCRIPTOR

Though this concept is simple in theory, complex descriptors are very easy to miss. This is because they look just like ordinary ACTION SENTENCES and IS SENTENCES. The only thing that differentiates them is the fact that they come directly after a general noun and the presence of an awkward pronoun. If you do not pay close attention, you may end up making the mistake of treating the complex descriptor as a new sentence:

$$\text{وَمَا مُحَمَّدٌ إِلَّا رَسُولٌ / قَدْ خَلَتْ مِن قَبْلِهِ الرُّسُلُ ... ﴿١٤٤﴾} \quad 3{:}144$$

Muhammad is only a messenger. Messengers have passed before him.

Use the following hints to make sure that you do not miss a complex descriptor:

1. Whenever you see a new sentence starting, throw a quick glance at the word before it. If it is general, you are looking at a complex descriptor. Make this a habit.

2. If you end up with a translation that sounds unnatural and choppy and consists of very short sentences, go back and check to make sure that you have not missed a complex descriptor.

MULTIPLE DESCRIPTORS

Recall that one word can have multiple descriptors. This applies to complex descriptors as well. A single word can have multiple complex descriptors or a combination or complex and normal descriptors.

$$\text{... بَشَرٌ [مِثْلُكُمْ] [يَأْكُلُ مِمَّا تَأْكُلُونَ مِنْهُ] ... ﴿٣٣﴾} \quad 23{:}33$$

...a man [like you] [who eats from what you eat from]...

$$\text{... قَوْمٍ [يُحِبُّهُمْ وَيُحِبُّونَهُ] [أَذِلَّةٍ عَلَى الْمُؤْمِنِينَ] [أَعِزَّةٍ عَلَى الْكَافِرِينَ] [يُجَاهِدُونَ فِي سَبِيلِ اللَّـهِ] ...﴿٥٤﴾} \quad 5{:}54$$

...a nation [who He loves and who love Him], [who are gentle with the believers] and [firm with the deniers], and [who fight in the path of Allah]...

☞ *Go to Chapter 25, Drill #3: Complex Descriptors in Context.*

COMPLEX DESCRIPTORS: when a full sentence is describing a noun

THE DESCRIBED

- will always be a general word

THE DESCRIPTOR

- will always be a full sentence
    - can be an *IS SENTENCE* or an *ACTION SENTENCE*
- will have an awkward pronoun
- will have a "who" or "that" or "which" in the translation

HOW TO SPOT

- whenever you see a new sentence, check to see if it is preceded by a general word
- if the translation sounds choppy, check to see if you missed a complex descriptor

OUR TERM	FORMAL TERM	ARABIC TERM
complex descriptor	sentence noun modifier	صِفَة مُشَبَّهَة

CHAPTER 26
THE EMPHASIZER مِنْ

INTRODUCTION

Compare the sentences on the right to the sentences on the left and observe how these sentences change in appearance and translation.

"God did not send a single messenger."

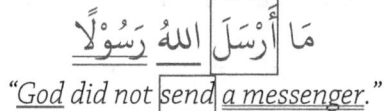
"God did not send a messenger."

"Not a single prophet came to us."

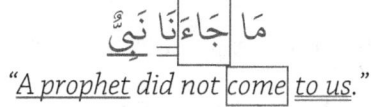
"A prophet did not come to us."

مَا لَنَا | مِنْ شُفَعَاءَ
"We do not have a single intercessor."

مَا لَنَا | شُفَعَاءُ
"We do not have any intercessors." (Lit, "For us are no intercessors.")

Notice the addition of مِنْ in each of the sentences on the left. The مِنْ has altered the word coming after it in a significant way: the words no longer have the labels that indicate their role. **<u>Yet their role in the sentence has not been altered! In translation, the only change was the additon of "not a single".</u>**

This is what we call the EMPHASIZER مِنْ. The EMPHASIZER مِنْ appears in negated sentences and translates as "not a single…" or "any…" It can appear before an AFTER IS, a DOER, or a RECEIVER. In the examples above, it appeared before the RECEIVER in the first sentence, before the DOER in the second, and before the AFTER IS in the third.

Much earlier, we learned that مِنْ is a TLDR word. The emphasizer مِنْ structure looks like a TLDR phrase. However, it does not translate like one. It translates according to its original role (AFTER IS, DOER, or RECEIVER), the only difference being the added emphasis.

Similar to the idea of the complex noun and the complex descriptor, the emphasizer مِنْ structure is a larger structure (a fragment or a sentence) playing the role of an ordinary noun. Let us learn how to spot the EMPHASIZER مِنْ and determine its role in a sentence.

THE EMPHASIZER مِنْ IN CONTEXT

An EMPHASIZER مِنْ can appear in negated sentences or question sentences. Let us start by looking at negated sentences, as it happens more often.

IN NEGATED SENTENCES

Remember that the EMPHASIZER مِنْ can appear before a DOER, RECEIVER, or AFTER IS. Also remember that it only appears in negated sentences. **<u>Always check to see if a sentence is negated before considering the possibility of an emphasizer مِنْ.</u>** This step is very important, because مِنْ appears as an ordinary TLDR very frequently in the Quran.

Once you have determined that you are looking at a negated sentence, the first step in narrowing down your options is to figure out what kind of sentence you are looking at.

- If you are looking at an IS SENTENCE, it must be the AFTER IS

- If you are looking at an ACTION SENTENCE, it can either be the DOER or RECEIVER

CLUES FOR ACTION SENTENCES

Use the following clues to arrive at the correct answer. These clues should look familiar as it is not our first time determining the role of a noun that does not display its label.

1. If the doer is embedded, there cannot be an outside doer. This means that the emphasizer مِنْ is the receiver.

14:4 ۝ ... وَمَا أَرْسَلْنَا مِن رَّسُولٍ إِلَّا [بِلِسَانِ قَوْمِهِ] ... ﴿٤﴾

We have not sent a single messenger except [with the language of his people]...

Since the action has an embedded doer (نحن), the emphasizer مِن can only be the receiver.

Also note how the مِن is translated. Had it been translated as a TLDR phrase, it would not have made sense, which is one way to know that it is an emphasizer مِن.

10:61 ۝ ... وَلَا تَعْمَلُونَ مِنْ عَمَلٍ إِلَّا كُنَّا [عَلَيْكُمْ] شُهُودًا إِذْ تُفِيضُونَ [فِيهِ] ... ﴿٦١﴾

You do not do a single action except that We are witnessing [you] as you do [it].

Since the action has an embedded doer (أنتم), the emphasizer مِن can only be the receiver.

Also note how the مِن is translated. Had it been translated as a TLDR phrase, it would not have made sense, which is one way to know that it is an emphasizer مِن.

2. Use common sense. Oftentimes, there is only one way a sentence makes sense.

6:59 ۝ ... وَمَا تَسْقُطُ مِن وَرَقَةٍ إِلَّا يَعْلَمُهَا ... ﴿٥٩﴾

Not a single leaf falls except that He knows about it.

Since the action "to fall" cannot take a receiver, the emphasizer مِن can only be the doer.

Also note how the مِن is translated. Had it been translated using its normal translation, it would not have made sense, which is one way to know that it is an emphasizer مِن.

CLUES FOR IS SENTENCES

In IS SENTENCES, the emphasizer مِن only ever appears on the AFTER IS. Once you have determined that the sentence is an IS SENTENCE, you already know what role the emphasizer مِن is playing.

Nevertheless, we will go over some additional hints that will help you spot the emphasizer مِنْ more quickly and easily.

1. When an emphasizer مِنْ appears in an *IS SENTENCE*, the sentence is made up of a string of TLDR phrases

2. The emphasizer مِنْ most often appears in sentences that denote belonging and start with the TLDR لِ, meaning "for".

7:65   ﴿ ٦٥ ﴾ ... مَا لَكُم | مِّنْ إِلَـٰهٍ غَيْرُهُ ...

You do not have <u>any God other than Him</u>.

Notice how the sentence is a string of TLDR phrases. Also note how the مِنْ is translated.

5:72   ﴿ ٧٢ ﴾ وَمَا لِلظَّالِمِينَ | مِنْ أَنصَارٍ ..

The oppressors will not have <u>any helpers</u>.

Notice how the sentence is a string of TLDR phrases. Also note how the مِنْ is translated.

26:100-101   فَمَا لَنَا | مِن شَافِعِينَ ﴿ ١٠٠ ﴾ وَلَا صَدِيقٍ حَمِيمٍ ﴿ ١٠١ ﴾

We do not have <u>any intercessors or close friends</u>.

Notice how the sentence is a string of TLDR phrases. Also note how the مِنْ is translated.

 Go to Chapter 26, Drill #1: In Negated Sentences.

IN QUESTION SENTENCES

Though the emphasizer مِنْ appears in negated sentences most often, it can also appear in question sentences. These questions are often rhetorical. Here are the question words that most often appear in combination with the emphasizer مِنْ.

كَأَيِّن مِنْ...	كَمْ مِنْ...	هَلْ مِنْ...
How many...?	How many...?	Are there any...at all?

Notice that there are كَمْ مِنْ and كَأَيِّن مِنْ translate the same way. They have the same meaning, the only difference being that كَأَيِّن is stronger and more emphatic. You may also have noticed that the emphasizer مِنْ is not captured in the translation of these two question words. This is simply because there is no natural way to capture the emphasis in translation. The implication that the مِنْ adds is that the answer to these rhetorical questions is "a lot."

Imagine, for example, that you are having a conversation with you friend and they say, "My reach is limited to Facebook users," and you respond by saying, "Well how many Facebook users do you think there are?" You are not literally asking them how many Facebook users there are. Rather, you are using this rhetorical question as another way of saying that there are a lot of Facebook users. Similarly, when a parent asks a child, "How many times did I tell you to clean your room?," it is not a literal question, but a way of saying that they have already asked many times. The usage of كَمْ مِنْ and كَأَيِّن مِنْ is similar to this.

... كَمْ مِّن فِئَةٍ قَلِيلَةٍ غَلَبَتْ فِئَةً كَثِيرَةً بِإِذْنِ اللَّـهِ ... ﴿٢٤٩﴾   2:249

How many small armies defeated large armies by the permission of Allah?

وَكَأَيِّن مِّنْ آيَةٍ فِي السَّمَاوَاتِ وَالْأَرْضِ يَمُرُّونَ عَلَيْهَا وَهُمْ عَنْهَا مُعْرِضُونَ ﴿١٠٥﴾   12:105

How many miracles are there in the skies and the earth that they pass by and give no heed to?

... قُلْ هَلْ مِنْ خَالِقٍ غَيْرُ اللَّـهِ يَرْزُقُكُم مِّنَ السَّمَاءِ وَالْأَرْضِ ... ﴿٣﴾   35:3

Say: is there **any** creator other than Allah who provides for you from the skies and the earth?

☞ *Go to Chapter 26, Drill #2: In Question Sentences.*

EXTRA مِنْ: used for emphasis. Translates as "any" or "not a single".

If you come across a مِنْ that does not make sense to translate in a normal way, think:

1. Is the sentence **NEGATED**? If it is, chances are that you have an emphasizer مِنْ.

    a) If it is an **IS SENTENCE**:

    → the sentence will be a **STRING OF TLDR** PHRASES

    → will often **BEGIN WITH POSSESSIVE** لِ

    b) If it is an **ACTION SENTENCE**

    → Is there an embedded doer? Or an outside doer with the doer label?

    ✓ If it is, then the مِنْ will be the receiver

    → What does the مِنْ fragment translate most naturally as?

2. Does it begin with هل،كم،كأين?

OUR TERM	FORMAL TERM	ARABIC TERM
emphasizer مِنْ	-	مِنْ الزَّائِدَة

MODULE 5: COMPLEX STRUCTURES

An examination of full sentences or fragments that act like nouns - nouns that are longer and more elaborate than ordinary nouns

COMPLEX NOUNS

complex noun + sentence*/TLD phrase*
will likely include an "awkward pronoun"

-**complex nouns**: الذي، التي، ما، أن
-can play any role in a sentence
-**doer**: if receiver role is occupied
-**substitute doer**: if it is after a passive
  if it comes after أن
-**receiver**: if action already has a doer
  (i.e., a word with doer label,
  commands, forbidding)
-**before is**: start of the sentence
-**after is**: later in the sentence

-can play a fragment level role:
-**descriptive**: if the noun before it is
  specific
-**possessive**: if the noun before it is
  general
-**TLD phrase**: right after a TLD word
-**sent. starter**: comes after a sent starter
  *remember: a TLD phrase can come
  between a sent. starter and its noun

ALWAYS CHECK TO SEE IF IT IS PLAYING
A FRAGMENT LEVEL ROLE FIRST!

COMPLEX DESCRIPTIONS

noun + a full sentence*
will likely include an "awkward pronoun"

Remember: when a new sentence starts,
spare a glance to the word before it: is it
a general noun? Then chances are you
have a complex descriptors.

Remember: if a translation does not sound
smooth, check to make sure that you did
not miss a complex descriptor

Translate: put a "which" or "who(m)"
between the noun and its description
(depending on whether it is human or not)

EMPHASIZER مِنْ

مِنْ + general noun
will be in a negated OR question sentence

Easiest way to identify an emphasizer مِنْ
is if translating the مِنْ in its normal way
does not make sense. Just make sure that:

-the sentence is negated OR question
-the noun coming before it is general

In an **action sentence**:
-can be a **doer or receiver**
-if an action already has a receiver, then
  it will be a doer, and vice versa

In an **is sentence**:
-it is easy to recognize because it will be in
  a sentence composed mostly of TLD
  phrases.

Translate: "not a single" or "any"

www.ingramcontent.com/pod-product-compliance
Lightning Source LLC
Chambersburg PA
CBHW080323080526
44585CB00021B/2453